PROJECT MANAGEMENT FOR SMBs

Gren Gale

One badly run project can leave your business fighting for its life

ZANNAC

BOOKS

Published by Zannac Books, United Kingdom, 2015

Edited and designed by Suzanna Cardash at Zanna C

Cover image © Osorioartist under license from dreamstime.com

Image on page 104 © Andrew Grossman under license from 123rf.com

Images on pages 18, 41, 46, 55 and 91 under license from shutterstock.com

A catalogue record for this book is recorded in the British Library

Kindle: ASIN B00RC2XFKG

ISBN 978 0 9928023 2 5 (UK edition)

ISBN 978 0 9928023 3 2 (US edition)

First published in print in 2014 using ISBN 978 15030243 3 5

To my children,

who are the diamonds that sparkle in my life

With many thanks to my amazing editor, Suzanna Cardash at Zanna C, who – with extraordinary patience! – helped to bring my words to life and designed the cover

CONTENTS

1. Introducing Projects

2. How to Deliver Projects

3. Project Governance

4. Soft Skills

5. Conclusion

1

INTRODUCING PROJECTS

Why do you need this book?

It's simple: a little discipline can prevent a potential crisis from taking your business down

Think your company's so small and focused that you can fudge project management issues and wing your way to success though charm, luck or prayer? Think again. In fact, project disciplines are as critical as financial ones for small businesses, if not more so.

While large organizations may find themselves licking their wounds after a project failure, it's unlikely to have a significant impact on their bottom line. For small companies, however, a project that costs significantly more than budgeted or takes longer to deliver can result in a crisis.

Anyone can run a project, but to deliver a high-quality product to time and budget requires leadership, skill and – as importantly – demands that your whole business is set up to support delivery.

In many cases smaller companies don't recognize that they're running projects. They simply see a discrete work task and get on with it. Actually, in some situations this is enough; but applying the principles described in this book will ensure that more of these pieces of 'work' are properly controlled, and finish on time and on budget.

Moreover, the organization, governance, people skills and professional approach to project management that are described here will give you a genuine competitive advantage over your rivals.

I'm not going to try to show you how to manage every shape and size of project. I'd need limitless pages! Neither is this book aimed at those controlling mega-programs with hundreds (or thousands) of staff, and millions to spend. Rather, we'll concentrate on how to manage projects where the spend isn't massive, but stakes are high.

Whether you're in charge of managing projects for your own company or someone else's, I'll show you the best way to run them in a smaller business. Moreover, I'll teach you how to do this whilst avoiding the mind-boggling bureaucracy that's endemic in large-company operations.

Additionally, I'll suggest ways of maintaining the rigor required to ensure that you can control and manage your projects effectively and efficiently.

Many small businesses find it impossible to justify employing dedicated, experienced project managers and, instead, charge existing employees (whose main role isn't – and perhaps never has been – project management) with coordinating multi-stranded projects. This is understandable, but it's a big ask. Let me help.

My aim is to provide support staff in such roles with an instant, off-the-shelf project delivery methodology that will work well for small and medium-sized companies, yet can easily be plugged into companies of any size.

This book is intended to offer guidance and suggest processes and the insight to avoid potential pitfalls. It should be an invaluable aid to professional project managers – and anyone else who's unexpectedly asked to run the show.

A salutary tale

A thriving company neglected to build a business case before charging into a major product development

A number of years ago I worked for a small company, at what was then the leading edge of technology. The business specialized in developing software and hardware and was doing pretty well.

We had our eyes on a top-end product that was being sold by a competitor for vastly more than our offering. In short, we believed it could be produced at a fraction of the cost, thus allowing us to clean up the market. Rather than looking at incremental development, we decided to cash in, and went straight for the top-end product.

Naturally, we estimated how long it would take us. New hardware and software had to be developed, but since both would be broadly based on what we'd designed already, we were pretty confident. On the basis of meetings with the developers, we reckoned we needed about six months to deliver the lower-priced product.

No organized estimation phase was undertaken, no risks were assessed and reviewed and no governance structure set up. There was no need, we reasoned, and the project got underway.

You've probably guessed the rest. Before long, the hardware development ran into difficulties and, needless to say, software development was dependent on the availability of the hardware.

Meanwhile, news that we were working on a new, better system was seeping out to customers, and sales started to fall off in anticipation. As a result, and while development issues persisted, we rushed to pour further investment into the new system, preparing its launch.

To cut to the chase, the company started to run into difficulties and was eventually sold – in a poor financial state – to a venture capital firm.

They bought the company because of the potential of the new product but naturally, they set about looking at ways of stemming losses. Layoffs began, further development was no longer viable and eventually the company was wound down and closed. The new product? It was never finished and never launched.

Why this riches to rags story? Well, with better attention to estimation, planning, risks and project disciplines this needn't have been the disaster it turned out to be. In fact, with a realistic view of costs and risks in front of them, the board might well have decided not to undertake this development at all, and launched a less risky and less ambitious product instead.

This was a case of a single project bringing a healthy and expanding company down, and it all came down to project disciplines. The words 'project' and 'late' don't have to be synonymous with one another if you train staff and put in place good governance and solid, repeatable project management processes.

So what's a 'project'?

Don't get on with 'work' without realizing you're running a project, and applying good project disciplines

Let's start at the beginning. How would I define a 'project'? How would you? It's an interesting question, as exemplified by the quotations below.

'The development of software for an improved business process, the construction of a building or bridge, the relief effort after a natural disaster, the expansion of sales into a new geographic market – all are projects. And all must be expertly managed to deliver the on-time, on-budget results, learning and integration that organizations need.'

Project Management Institute

'A project is a temporary endeavor undertaken to create, modify, or retire a unique product, service, or result. A project has a definite start and end date and concludes when its objectives have been achieved.'

Harvard Graduate School of Education

'A temporary organization that is created for the purpose of delivering one or more business products according to an agreed Business Case.'

PRINCE2

You get the idea. The common theme is that projects a) deliver change in some form or another, b) have defined start and end points and c) come in on budget.

I'd throw in another element, too: that projects are collaborative activities where teamwork and communication are hugely important. In order to deliver, successful project managers must be able to lead, engage, coordinate and empathize with all the various individuals and groups involved.

Project Managers

Do all projects need a Project Manager? The short answer is yes! Many only require one part-time but in my experience, projects do tend to drift when nobody assumes overall responsibility and carries the can. The team will fail to keep monitoring risks or fight for resources because they have other tasks to carry out, and the project will gently but surely slip down the priority list.

As project manager you'll run the show and will be responsible for delivering to the specified budget, plan and quality while keeping project staff and stakeholders happy. It's not an easy job and requires patience, determination, persistence as well as the ability to absorb facts and then make decisions.

It can also be very rewarding. You are in charge, after all, so to a large extent your fate is in your own hands. Run projects well and you'll be a hero; run them badly and the reverse is true. This book will provide you with the ammunition needed to ensure you fall into the former camp.

2

HOW TO DELIVER PROJECTS

The project delivery process

You don't need to apply complex project management methodologies to achieve successful deliveries – honest!

If your company's relatively small, why make life more complicated than it needs to be? As the old adage goes, you wouldn't crack a nut with a sledgehammer. The vast majority of projects can be broken down into eight stages:-

Business Case
Come up with the idea and agree the business case

Start-up
Start the project

Analysis
Work out and agree *what* the requirements are

Design
Think out *how* you will deliver the requirements

Build
Build what's needed to deliver those requirements

Test
Test it to make sure it works and performs

Implement
Move the change from development into the real world

Closure
Close the project and try to work out what you could have done better

There are different ways of arranging and organizing these stages (see page 66 on Agile methodologies), but you'll go through them in one form or another in just about every project.

The process is shown pictorially overleaf and, more often than not in the real world, the stages shown overlap.

PMP and PRINCE2 are the two popular project management methodologies that predominate worldwide. However, both were designed to manage huge programs of work rather than the challenges that face those of us running smaller businesses.

My hands-on experience of running large numbers of projects in the real world has enabled me to pick out the facets of PMP and PRINCE2 that work best in organizations with fewer people and more modest resources. This won't just make your life easier, but will enable you to reap financial benefits via the reduction of unnecessary overheads.

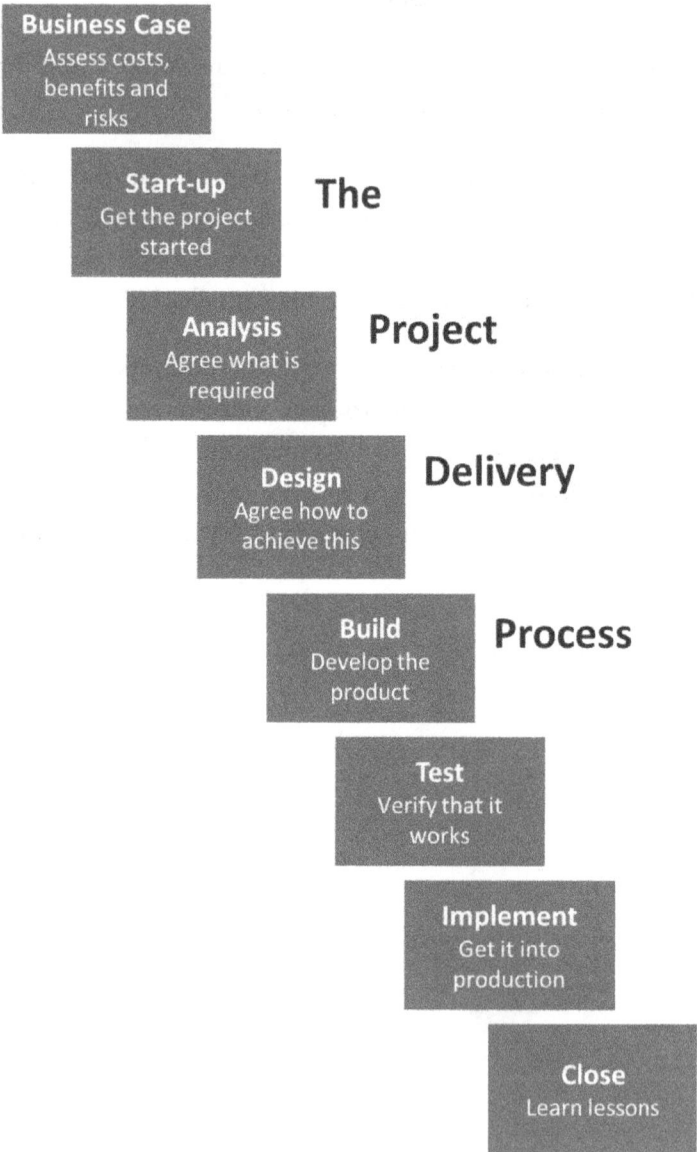

The

Project

Delivery

Process

- **Business Case** — Assess costs, benefits and risks
- **Start-up** — Get the project started
- **Analysis** — Agree what is required
- **Design** — Agree how to achieve this
- **Build** — Develop the product
- **Test** — Verify that it works
- **Implement** — Get it into production
- **Close** — Learn lessons

Business Case

If you don't understand Scope, Benefits and Costs, how can you deliver on time or budget?

In fact, let's take this a step further. If you haven't covered the basics, how can you know if your project's worth doing in the first place?

Let's assume you're at the Business Case stage. First off, you need to get a handle on what you want the project to deliver (the scope), why you're doing it (the benefits), what it's going to cost and how long it's going to take to deliver (the costs).

Is it really so important to collate all this information when it's only a rough idea? Absolutely!

Gut instinct and your knowledge of the marketplace are obviously good starting points too, but establishing a project without basic business information is like setting off on an Antarctic expedition wearing a fleece jacket and a pair of sneakers. Don't be surprised if things get a bit slippery before long.

Once you've got all the information you need you'll have the components of a business case and can make a start or, where relevant, meet with senior management to agree whether or not to embark on the journey.

I know the concept of 'business cases' smacks of internal developments and product companies. Perhaps you don't usually originate project proposals but bid for work put out to tender by other organizations.

Rest assured that the principles can be applied equally well to service companies. If you're hoping to manage a project for someone else's company and can't prove the work will a) be profitable, b) can be done when the customer wants it and c) has an acceptable level of risk, you shouldn't be bidding for it.

Inputs to this stage	• The project idea
Actions within this stage	• Define project's scope to a level that allows you to estimate costs • Produce cost estimates • Produce an outline plan • Produce a business case • Gain approval to proceed from your senior management
Outputs from this stage	• Outline definition of project scope • Business Case • Approval to proceed

Your Business Case should be a document – usually a set of slides – that puts together all work carried out at this stage in a way that can be presented to senior management for approval. If it's your business or you're the senior manager, it will be an invaluable starting point that will crystallize your thinking.

It should contain:

- A summary of scope

- Benefits

- Cost estimates

- An outline plan

- Major assumptions and dependencies

- Major risks

The Business Case should be approved by key decision-makers before you move to the next stage of the project. Moreover, this approval should represent their absolute commitment; it's not just a box-ticking exercise. After all, if the project is to succeed, it must have their full backing.

Scope

You'll have to expand the scope beyond initial ideas. 'Build a new website' doesn't cut it because it's woolly and has no parameters. In short, you can't produce estimates from a statement like that.

First, try to express the project idea as a single statement that describes a clear objective. This should give a clear but high-level view of what needs to be delivered and, where there could be doubt, what isn't going to be delivered. So rather than 'Build a new website,' you could say 'Replace our existing website with one that's modern, more responsive, much easier to change and supports the sale of our products on-line.'

You'll then need to expand this into a series of more detailed statements that will allow you to produce rough costings.

The best way to achieve this is to run a workshop. A one-day session will usually do the trick but in many cases you'll need less time and in some you may need more. It depends on the size of the project.

In essence, you need to bring together the people who know what's required with those who'll actually be developing the change and can estimate its costs.

This will give the developers a better understanding of what's being suggested and allow them to ask questions you may not have considered. As importantly, it will enable them to advise on areas where a slightly different approach might deliver the same benefit at a lower cost.

This process should result in a series of single-line statements outlining what's planned. Full requirements will be produced during the Analysis stage, so make sure you resist the temptation to go into too much detail at this point. For our mythical website build, suitable statements might be:-

1. The home page must show clear navigation, and must make a real impact and draw people in

2. All pages must load within a maximum of 3 seconds

3. Web pages must be easy to change by non-IT staff

4. All company promotions must be featured on or have links from the home page

5. The company's products must be shown on dedicated product pages

6. Products must be searchable by a number of keys

7. These products must be categorized by type

8. There must be a facility to purchase products online by debit or credit card or PayPal

9. Customers must be able to register for a 'your account' facility

10. There must be a wish list or favourites facility for customers' reference

11. We need 'About us' and 'Terms and Conditions' pages

12. The website must be linked to a third party package to carry out order processing, inventory control and returns handling.

This sort of detail may or may not be enough for the estimators present on the day, but during the workshop you should find the right level. Clearly they have to be confident that they know enough about the proposal to be capable of doing their job for you.

To help them, it's useful to think about the business value of each requirement and set basic priority levels for each. High, medium or low should be enough.

Estimation and planning

Estimation is one of the most important parts of any project. Get it wrong and the whole business case may become invalid as the project progresses; costs can start to exceed benefits.

Worse still, escalating project costs that are running out of control in a small or medium business may become a threat to the financial stability of the entire company.

Estimation and planning go hand in hand and become a collaborative team job. As Project Manager you need to coordinate the two, certainly, but if the teams who will be doing the work don't produce their own estimates, they'll feel no ownership or commitment to them. You may have to help if they're not used to doing this – in fact, I'd encourage you to do so if that's the case – but please resist the temptation to impose your estimates on them.

"Can we make a billion widgets in one week?"

There are plenty of estimation techniques, but all of them centre on breaking the project down into smallish components. This ensures that the project team feels comfortable about estimating; plus, of course, each individual estimate is likely to be more accurate.

The technique is often referred to as producing a 'work breakdown' structure; that is, decomposing all the work required into a tree of components, the bottom leaves of which are small enough to estimate. Our aforementioned website project might look a bit like the one on the next couple of pages.

Work Breakdown

1. <u>Home Page</u>

    a. Design impactful look and feel

    b. Build menu system

    c. Show promotions

    d. Show contact details

    e. Show shopping basket

2. <u>Three-second load time</u>

    a. Optimize code

    b. Plan for performance testing

    c. Build performance testing environment

3. <u>Web pages must be easy to change by non-IT staff</u>

    a. Build page editor

    b. Build functionality to let users test pages before go-live

    c. Devise user control structure

    d. Build user control

4. Promotions page

    a. Links from home page

    b. Build links to products page

    c. Build functionality to provide options for sliders and static images/text

    d. Build functionality to be able to show images and text

…and so on, until you have covered all of the scope statements.

The example given shows you the principle, but if you were really producing estimates to build the site you'd probably continue to break down components. Eventually you'd reach a level of granularity, or small details, that would give estimators the ability to produce good estimates.

The beauty of the work breakdown structure is that you can review it with the whole estimation team to check nothing's been missed.

Separating the estimate down into small chunks will also lead to increased accuracy. Mistakes in small numbers tend to have less impact than mistakes in large ones – it's sometimes referred to as the 'law of small numbers'.

Encourage your estimation teams to continue talking to the business and its customers during the process, to avoid misunderstandings.

It's also worth asking them discuss any scenarios where costs might be lowered if a slightly different approach was taken.

You can (and should) challenge and question other people's estimates, but never – ever! – provide estimates for work that other employees are going to carry out. It's as simple as that.

Estimates checklist

The keys to success in estimating? Make sure you constantly challenge what you're told, and think realistically about productivity.

People are, on the whole, optimistic and keen to please. This means they're likely to underestimate, especially if they have little experience in this field. That's why it's important for you, as Project Manager, to challenge their figures and timescales and make sure that they've considered all eventualities.

What other tasks are entrusted to the team who will carry out the work? Do these people also have to answer phones, meet customers or suppliers or support other projects? Someone might, justifiably, declare that something will take just five days to complete, but how much elapsed time will that translate into when you take into account all of their other responsibilities?

It's also easy to be caught out by essential work that the whole team knows needs doing: everyone assumes that someone else must have discussed it or offered the information. Estimators are just as likely to make numerous other assumptions too, that they mysteriously fail to mention. Why? Because from their point of view, they seem so obvious! You may find they're counting on the fact that equipment, software or office space will be there for you. Has anyone actually asked the right questions about these? What if they're unavailable?

Additionally, don't forget to list what you might need to buy for your project. People's time will be one of your costs, but do you need to buy in components, software, equipment, training or transport?

You'll need to track your spend as the project progresses, but it's also a good idea to track how well individual estimators do against actuals. Then, the next time you ask them to estimate, you will know whether they're optimistic or realistic estimators, and can add contingencies accordingly.

Don't forget that you'll need to estimate for each of the stages shown in this book, not just the Build stage. You'll also have to estimate for the project management effort.

Put a lot of work into estimation and your outline plan. As often as not, everyone involved is in a big hurry to get the show on the road and wants to get this phase done and dusted.

Pause, take a deep breath and remember that senior managers are unlikely to be impressed by changes in costs and timeframes once the project is underway.

Time spent at the start of the project will always pay dividends later, so try as far as possible to resist pressure to 'just get started'.

Abraham Lincoln had the right idea. In one of his more famous quotes he purportedly said 'Give me six hours to chop down a tree and I will spend the first four sharpening the axe.'

Estimates for outsourced work

If you need to get estimates for outsourced work, the best you'll be able to achieve at this stage is a budgetary estimate. Of course, it's unlikely to be accurate and, in my experience, it's likely to be a lot lower than the final quote.

This is hardly surprising. The last thing suppliers want to do is frighten you off with too high a quote; hence there's a natural tendency to provide a low one, caveated as 'budgetary'. You won't be able to get a reliable figure until you can provide them with detailed requirements, and you won't have those until the Analysis stage.

So unless you know, trust and have worked extensively with a particular supplier before, I recommend adding a contingency of at least 20% to any estimate you get at this point.

Contingency

Carefully consider contingency, both for costs and planning.

A risk-based approach is an effective way of estimating anything that can be influenced by chance. Work out your major risks, think through the implications of what would happen if those risks were to become issues, and then calculate how much contingency you need to mitigate them.

Beware of senior management who tell you to remove contingency on the grounds that the business case isn't viable if it's included.

In my experience, giving way to this pressure usually spells disaster further down the line. I've *never* run a project where everything went exactly as expected and I doubt you ever will, either. You need contingency; it's not just an optional extra.

You'll want to think about how you use it, of course. It can make sense to keep a slice of contingency for the project manager to control. Secure in the knowledge that you're equipped with extra resources, you can try pushing estimators to stick to their original figures. Then, if this really proves impossible, you'll still have money in your back pocket.

This counters the natural tendency for a project to expand to fit not just the allotted estimated figures, but the contingency fund as well.

Audit trail

Senior management will need to be reassured that estimates for a project have been decided in a professional manner, so keep an audit trail of how you got there. Cost data from previous projects can be useful in justifying your decisions, but in the end it's about building confidence. A logical trail will enable you to justify why the estimates you're presenting represent a good assessment of the costs.

Elephants are hard to swallow in one go

People get carried away with the excitement of new projects, especially when they involve product launches. As a result, too many people want to wade in for the full scope from day one.

Throw in a bit too much optimism about the delivery date and you can end up juggling a product development that's out of control, as well as appointments with the bank manager and sleepless nights.

The bigger the project gets, the greater the pressure to reduce cost estimates and deliver fast, which of course adds exponentially to the probability of getting it wrong.

It won't come as a shock to learn that the larger a project becomes, the harder it is to control. Big projects are inherently risky and rarely deliver on time and on budget. Government is teeming with examples of mismanaged projects that were unfeasibly big but had to be delivered before a coming election, so went ahead anyway... and failed miserably.

Less ambitious projects, however, are a lot more successful. So if possible, try to split a big project into a number of less weighty ones, each of which delivers something you can release into production.

Smaller projects aren't just easier and less stressful to manage. They also deliver functionality earlier, giving you more flexibility to react to market changes and allowing greater scope for collaborative working between a business, its customers and developers.

Splitting a project into smaller components can sometimes appear difficult or even impossible at first, and is likely to stretch the overall timeframe out. However, since it's generally recognized that large projects hardly ever deliver on time, the stretch is usually illusory; and besides, the gains you make from the split will make it worthwhile.

Planning

Once you have your estimates you'll need to produce an outline plan, organized according to the stages detailed in this book.

It needn't be too detailed but must, of course, be deliverable. Take care not to overload resources, include timescale contingency, and work out what the dependencies will be between the tasks, any third parties and yourselves.

There is a lot more on planning on page 34.

Assumptions and dependencies

We've already covered the dangers of assumptions when estimating, but sometimes they're unavoidable.

Realistically, it's likely that the teams producing initial estimates will have to make at least some assumptions about certain aspects of scope or design, given the relatively thin knowledge of requirements at this stage.

As Project Manager, you too may need to make assumptions, for example about a particular resource being available when necessary. The project may also be dependent on external events outside its immediate control, such as a deliverable from another project.

It's not unusual to have assumptions and dependencies, but it's crucial that the project manager emphasizes these when presenting estimates and plans.

Why? Because senior managers and customers will naturally pay more attention to the stated timeline and costs than to your assumptions and dependencies.

However, if, in the future, these assumptions prove false and dependencies aren't satisfied, costs and delivery dates are prone to increase – and it's important that they understand this from the outset.

Risks

Try to quantify the big risks threatening the project at this stage. Examples at this level would be:-

- You don't understand things well enough yet to be confident about your estimates

- A competitor could launch a rival product before you can get to market

- You might be unable to get the specialist staff required.

Benefits

Too many projects get underway without a full appraisal of the benefits of undertaking them, and whether they're worth pursuing. You're likely to want to make money, save money or both in return for the time and effort you put into a project.

Benefits are sometimes hard to quantify because they come in all sorts of shapes and sizes. Financial return should be relatively easy to calculate – is there a direct monetary benefit, in terms of profit or saving? - but there are often less tangible advantages such as academic acclaim, good PR or reaching a new audience.

Intangible benefits can also include improved service and enhanced customer retention and satisfaction, but it's prudent to look ahead, too. You may, for example, have to insist that the team implements design elements that will enable the company to avoid a fine.

Few of us would want to risk litigation, potential criminal charges or even imprisonment for the sake of profit, so never, *ever* underestimate the intangible benefits of *not* getting sued.

Those who put this maxim to the test soon discover that the results of a lost court case become remarkably tangible and long-lasting in the eyes of customers and potential customers alike.

It's not uncommon to see benefits inflated in a desperate attempt to make the business case work, but this is commercially naïve and does nobody any favours. It's just a way of delaying the final reckoning. If you don't think you can sell enough of a proposed new product to justify its costs, it's time to stop and look at something else.

Whatever you are doing, the costs need to be justified in some way and if they can't be justified, you shouldn't be doing the project.

Bidding for work as a service company

Is your role in a service-providing business that bids to win work?

Actually, getting your pitch together is not unlike producing a business case for an internal investment.

In both cases, you're attempting to convince a customer that they should invest in developing whatever it is that they want – and in you.

Either way, your response will be built around what the customer wants, and it's vital that you:-

- Provide a written response

- Understand the scope to a sufficient depth to produce good estimates. Don't be shy about asking the customer questions if anything's unclear – this is your neck on the line

- Make clear what you understand to be in the scope and, as importantly, what you've assumed is not

- Fully understand your own costs, particularly your staff costs (or you won't be able to calculate if your bid price will make a profit)

- Only consider bidding a fixed price at this stage if the customer's requirements are well defined (or you are risking grief and possible financial disaster later)

- Carefully review estimates, timeframes, levels of contingency, risks, assumptions and dependencies before submitting the bid

- Clarify to your customer what assumptions and dependencies you have made in producing your quote

- Are not afraid to turn business down if you conclude that the risks are too great or profit margin too low to consider bidding

- Make sure to cost in support for the customer's acceptance test and that you define exit criteria (unless you want your customer to assume all faults will be fixed, no matter how minor, before the product can be accepted)

- Either state that no warranty is included or make sure you cost for it

- Make clear what the customer's responsibilities will be in the project.

Why business cases matter

If you find the prospect of all this estimating and benefit measurement a bit tiresome, I suggest you have a chat with one of the original investors in the rail tunnel linking England to France – the Channel Tunnel. Yep, the ones who saw their investment decimated and even the promise of the free use of the tunnel removed. How come? Simple. Their business case turned out to be badly flawed.

Okay, let's cut them some slack. Clearly this would have been an extremely arduous business case to put together. It's not as though someone else had already dug a tunnel under that stretch of sea, on which they could base their estimates, so there would have been countless unknowns and risks as well as a whole lot of politics.

We could speculate for hours on how their estimate was phrased, but the fact is that the tunnel delivered a year late and 80% over budget. Since this changed the basis of the original business case, the unfortunate (or short-sighted) company operating the tunnel had to raise passenger charges to try to pay off the debt. It didn't work too well, because fares were then so expensive that no-one was using the tunnel...

Everyone involved was hit by a perfect storm of overly optimistic development costs and revenue forecasts, and an inadequate assessment of risk.

Bankruptcy loomed, but in the end the issue was solved by financial restructuring, which meant giving a lot of the company away to their creditors and diluting the existing shareholder ownership. I'm sure the guys putting the original business case together believed they'd done a good job, but they didn't quite make the grade.

The Channel Tunnel was a multi-billion dollar enterprise and, if you're reading this book, yours probably isn't – yet! However, the principles are just as relevant to SMBs, whether you're undertaking projects in the hundreds, or hundreds of thousands: if the project goes wrong, the consequences can be severe.

Fundamentally, the tunnel was a sound idea. It opened in 1994, is still operating and is now making money. But after a big mistake, the same might not be true for your business; so make sure you don't make one.

Start-up

Get your project organized as soon as possible and make sure everyone knows what they're meant to be doing

You won't be surprised to learn that this stage formally starts the project and lets everyone know the show is on the road.

Inputs to this stage	• Outline definition of the project scope • Business Case • Approval to proceed
Actions within this stage	• Project Sponsor appointed • Project Manager appointed • Project Sponsor and Project Management agree who should be members of Project Board • Project Initiation Document (PID) produced • More detailed Project Plan produced
Outputs from this stage	• PID • Project Plan

The Project Sponsor and Project Board

These are key roles in the project and demand your best players.

The Project Sponsor will ultimately be responsible for the whole thing, and his or her strength and support will have a big influence on its success. The Project Board, meanwhile, is the executive committee that will steer the project.

In a modestly sized company the Project Sponsor might well be the company owner and the Project Board may be very small, though having at least three people (including the Project Sponsor) is usually a good idea.

As a minimum, the Board should contain a Senior User and an internal Senior Supplier. The user will be someone who owns the deliverables or end products of this project (sometimes referred to as the Product Owner); the supplier will be the person responsible for delivery and might, for example, be a Head of Change or of an IT function.

Ultimately, however, the Board's size doesn't really matter. What's important is that everyone's clear who owns the project, and who has an interest in it being delivered; and that these people meet regularly to guide and support the project.

A critical factor that's often overlooked is that those appointed need to be truly committed to success, and must really buy into the idea.

I've worked on projects where the sponsor has been press-ganged into the job and, as a result, has carried out the role half-heartedly. This, as you'd expect, makes the Project Manager's job a lot tougher.

Uncommitted Project Sponsors aren't just the preserve of large companies; they're equally prevalent in small companies where, being busy individuals, they stay at arm's length, and only start to pay attention when a part of the project goes wrong. By then, it's often too late.

The Sponsor and Board's roles are to challenge and support the Project Manager – as well as the project itself – from the outset.

The Board, in particular, needs to be mindful that success is ultimately their responsibility, so they must do everything in their power to facilitate this. They're part of the assurance mechanism that makes sure the Project Manager can work effectively, and that the project stays on track.

Did you know that the CHAOS report from the Standish Group indicated that around 10% of projects fail because of lack of executive support? You do now.

Project Initiation Document

I promised you less bureaucracy at the start of this book and this probably feels like more rather than less, but bear with me.

A Project Initiation Document (PID) is really worth producing because it's the only place where the whole project is described in a single document.

On reading it, anyone joining the team will be able to understand what's going on. It's also an excellent checklist for you, as the Project Manager, since it will help to make sure you've thought everything through. It needs to detail:

- How the project will be carried out

- The structure of the project team

- Who has what responsibilities

- The plan and milestones

- How quality will be controlled

- How change will be controlled

- What communication will be carried out during the project.

As discussed earlier, time and effort spent at the start will reduce the risk of disasters later. Small omissions and errors in initial thinking can turn into much bigger issues further down the line, so it's really worth investing in your PID to give yourself a smoother time later in the project.

In many ways it's a written Project Plan as opposed to the Project Schedule that most people will commonly refer to as 'the plan'.

It needn't be the length of the entire works of Shakespeare. In fact, it might not be as long as one short play! You should tailor the PID to the size of your particular enterprise.

Project Plan

As soon as your project is underway you're going to need to start adding more detail to the outline Project Plan you produced for your Business Case. And to do this, you're going to need a project planning tool.

Don't underestimate the impact of a good project planning tool on your ability to manage projects. A good planning tool will allow you to produce, modify and share plans, capture time worked and compare your estimates against what actually happened. It should also have good reporting facilities to allow project managers and business owners to understand what's happening in their projects at the press of a button.

Many tools also offer collaboration facilities to allow staff to share, review and comment on plans and documents, as well as providing chat boards and instant messaging. A bit like Facebook and Twitter combined, but for work, not play.

Collaboration packages work particularly well for geographically dispersed teams and for projects where there are subcontractors, clients, or both, who you want to engage more closely with the project.

This is however quite a confusing marketplace with over two hundred project management tools on offer at the time of writing. Most suppliers offer free trials or give away cut down versions of their products. The word free is very seductive, but don't imagine this is charity or generosity. Vendors know that once you start using their software, you'll invest time in training, implementing standards for using it and so on, until you get to the point that you've invested so much time, you won't want to change.

So what should you choose?

If you don't have a budget, then **ProjectLibre,** rated 'Best of Open Source' in 2013, is a nice simple project planning tool that will help you to produce plans in **Gantt** format (the bar charts commonly used for project plans). If you want to research and try similar free tools you'll find a useful guide at *opensource.com*.

However if you can afford to invest then there are some exceptional packages available. At the low end, **Rational Plan** is a comprehensive project planner that doesn't cost a lot of money. **Rational Plan** is a package that has to be installed on your PC or local server (although they are also testing a cloud based version). If you want a cloud based mid-priced planning and collaboration tool then **EasyProjects** is hard to beat, with everything I'd expect to see in this type of project management package. **Rational Plan** has a single one off charge, **EasyProjects**, as for all cloud based packages, has a monthly charge. For a limited time, the vendors of **Rational Plan** and **EasyProjects** have been kind enough to offer a 10% discount to readers of this book. See details on page 141.

Take your time to select and try out any packages that meet your needs, because once you've chosen a tool and started using it, you'll find it hard to swap to a different one.

Once the right one has been trialled, chosen and installed, you can start building your Project Plan, including all the stages we've covered in earlier sections.

These plans are always fluid documents at the beginning, but as your project progresses and you fully understand its requirements, it should become very solid. Once the design is finished and agreed, the plan should be baselined – by which I mean complete – and will show delivery dates you know you can meet.

The nearer an activity is on the plan, the more detail it should contain. As a rule of thumb, the next month's activities should be planned down to chunks of no longer than two weeks' duration apiece. Going forward from there, plans may be less detailed.

They must obviously show deliverables and dependencies and should be constructed around the resources you have available. Take a realistic view of when they will be free and what their availability is likely to be.

For example, if staff are involved in other activities, such as support work, they won't be at your call at all times. A variety of overheads will also affect availability, such as vacation, sickness, staff meetings and training.

Bear in mind, too, that resources consist of more than people. If you don't have a room big enough for your team, you may not be able to get your project off the ground; and if no testing environment is available, then you won't be able to test a system. I could go on…

Allow for lead times, too. Finding all resources is likely to take time and they'll have to be integrated into the project gradually, rather than on the same day. If you're hiring or buying equipment, contact the manufacturer for information on stock levels in advance.

Parts of your plan will usually be delegated to suppliers or team leads. Ask your supplier to provide a plan with milestones but don't merge this plan with yours; just include the milestones.

You can also expect to delegate parts of the plan to technical teams. This could, for example, be for process development, IT development or testing. In most cases you can delegate the detailed planning to the leads in those technical areas and, as above, include the milestones from their plans in yours.

Suppliers and team leaders alike need to understand that it's their responsibility to deliver to the plans they have provided.

Project start-up meeting

Never forget that any project is a collaborative activity. Whether you're running a project with in-house resources or outsourced suppliers, this principle remains true.

As Project Manager you're there to facilitate and co-ordinate this collaboration, so remember that at the start of the project you need to get all members of the team together – from developers, testers and suppliers to prospective users – to walk through all the information in the PID.

This will be partly for their information, and partly so you can get their feedback.

It also makes sense to ask the Senior User or Product Owner to present their case at this meeting, to ensure that everyone involved understands the objective of the project as well as the end product.

More simply still, they must know exactly what they're trying to build, and why, if the project's to be successful.

Analysis

If you can't define your requirements, you don't know what you're trying to achieve

At this stage you'll be defining the details of exactly what is wanted. The CHAOS report from the Standish Group indicated that an eye-popping 25% of projects fail because the people involved haven't categorically agreed on what's required. In other words, it's very, very important to do this carefully.

Inputs to this stage	• PID • Project Plan
Actions within this stage	• Carry out analysis to capture and document requirements • Get requirements reviewed and signed off • Carry out a Risk Review • Review estimates and plans in light of the agreed requirements • Hold a Project Board meeting at the end of this stage
Outputs from this stage	• Requirements definition • Documented risks

Another vital aspect (that often gets forgotten by managers eager to jump the gun) is this: if you ask a supplier for a quote without defining your requirements, you're likely to get your fingers burned.

Requirements capture

Some of the biggest project disasters come from having poor or incomplete requirements. This makes sense. After all, if you don't know exactly what's needed, how can you possibly deliver it on time and on budget?

Don't panic, because producing them need not be a complex process. Typically, requirements are captured as individual statements of a line each in a spreadsheet. You'll have a starting point in the outline requirements that were collected at the Business Case stage.

You need to make them clear and unambiguous but don't overload the requirements or go into too much detail. You'll flesh out the details later, during Design, and won't want to constrain the developers too much at this stage.

You may wish to write out simple statements of functionality, such as, 'There must be a function to take membership payments online', or you may want to produce these in what are usually referred to as user stories, such as 'As a member, I want an online membership payment function so that it's simpler to pay for my annual membership.' The generalized form of user stories is 'As a **<role>** I want **<goal or action>** to achieve **<benefit>**.'

It's not unusual for too many requirements to be specified, making it impossible for all of them to be implemented within the time or budget available. It's therefore useful to classify needs according to priority, or as 'musts', 'shoulds' or 'coulds'. This makes it easier to defer the less important requirements and agree an implementation order if the project needs to be split into smaller chunks.

"Seems like the Computer Analyst is taking his job just a little too literally"

Try to avoid 'nice to have' requirements. All requirements cost money and your objective is to design and deliver something fit for purpose. Include too many pleasing non-essentials and you may find your budget running out of control without much value being added.

The Senior User/Product Owner, or someone they delegate this to, should review and sign off the requirements so that there can be no disagreements down the line as to what was agreed to be delivered.

You'll also need to document less obvious 'non-functional requirements' such as performance, resilience, security, disaster recovery and back-ups. These could be critical, especially where an IT system is concerned.

Once all items are agreed and signed off, they need to be change-controlled so that any proposed amendments are raised as formal Change Requests, and their costs and benefits assessed. Only then can they can be approved. Normally the Project Board will have to approve Change Requests (see page 95 on Change Control).

Outsourcing

This is so fundamental that it's worth repeating: if you're outsourcing work, always finalize your requirements before asking suppliers to tender, so both you and they know exactly what you're being quoted for.

Asking for prices and delivery dates for a vague requirement helps neither party. I've come across lots of examples of buyers and suppliers falling out over poor 'requirements' where the supplier, in good faith, quoted for something that wasn't what the buyer eventually wanted.

Review estimates and plans

Once requirements are finalized you should review the estimates and plans you produced for the Business Case.

Project Boards and Sponsors will be extremely unimpressed by increases in costs or timeframe once the project is underway, particularly where the Sponsor owns the company and can see his or her money rapidly disappearing.

If costs increase as a result of this review, one option is to show how the project can still be delivered as planned if some of the lower priority requirements are deferred.

It's also essential to maintain your audit trail so you can demonstrate where and why costs have increased.

This is particularly important in smaller companies, where you may need to reassure the Sponsor and Project Board (or customer, if you're in a service company) that the project isn't out of control.

Risk Review

Once requirements are clear, there should be a much better understanding of likely risks and issues. A Risk Review, as detailed on page 92, will enable you to document the threats.

Project Board

You're almost ready to get down to business at this stage. Armed with better estimates and plans, you should call a meeting of the Project Board, to ask for all documentation to be approved.

You may have to explain an increase in costs and/or timescales or get agreement to deferring some non-essential requirements, but your clear and carefully thought-out substantiating explanations should make this a lot easier to justify.

Producing requirements as a service company

If you're part of a service company it's wise to avoid providing a cost or timescale unless you have clear requirements from your customer. When forced to provide some sort of quote, make sure you emphasize that it's only budgetary and can't be confirmed until you are given clear requirements.

It may turn out that the first job you're asked to undertake, as a supplier, is analyzing and documenting your customer's requirements. You can, of course, offer to document the scope on a time and materials basis, thus enabling you to provide a fixed price.

If you find yourself producing requirements on your customer's behalf, try to not see yourself in the lesser role of order-taker. Since the cost of the project will naturally be important to them (and could make or break their decision to award you the contract to carry it out), do your best to show how you can help them to deliver within their budget.

It's important to make sure that clients prioritize their requirements, and you can add value by pointing out requests that could be very expensive to implement. Where appropriate, you can also suggest alternatives which are likely to cost a lot less; this will gain their trust and confirm that you have their best interests at heart.

Once the deal is agreed, it's worth organizing a walkthrough of each item with your customer, including costs and timescales, to make sure they completely understand everything that is or isn't included, and when it will be delivered.

Most importantly, always make sure that your customer signs off these requirements, so there's no room for doubt about what he or she has agreed to pay for.

Design

Would you build a house or car without designing it? Thought not. Think before you jump in and 'just do it'

This stage defines the details of *how* project requirements will be achieved without culminating in an expensive mess.

What's a design?

A design is a detailed definition of how requirements will be implemented.

This could be drawings and a written specification if you're producing a building; a functional specification describing exactly how the system will function for an IT development; or high-level processes, an operating model and a design document if you're setting up a new business processing department.

Who does the designing?

The design will typically be created by experts in whatever it is you are building or changing.

If you're outsourcing this work, your chosen supplier will draw up designs on your behalf, but make sure they allow you to review these. You're the client and are paying, so you must ensure that you get what you want.

Projects carried out using or partially using the Agile methodology (see page 66) may not have a defined design stage. Instead, users will run design, build and test iterations, usually referred to as Sprints.

In Agile, timeframes and effort are baselined rather than designs, with an agreed number of Sprints built into the project and functionality constrained by the time available.

"The wheel was great. But what have you done for me lately?"

Cross-referencing

It's very easy to miss out requirements when completing a design. To make sure you don't omit anything, create a spreadsheet on which each customer requirement is listed alongside the part of the design that addresses it. This will provide you with an invaluable checklist that shows you've covered everything. It won't take long to compile and could save an embarrassing situation further down the line.

Design review

It's a good idea to hold Design review meetings, particularly where lots of design components are coming together. Passing documents around for review via email runs the risk of you – or someone else – missing a vital point about how the jigsaw will fit together.

When the design has been reviewed it should be signed off by the Senior User/Product Owner, unless they have delegated this task.

Once this is out of the way, the design needs to be change-controlled. That means that any proposed alterations will have to be raised as formal change requests, and their costs and benefits assessed, before they can be approved. Normally the Project Board will approve change requests (see page 95 on Change Control).

Test Strategy

Just as the Design shows how you're going to implement requirements, the Test Strategy shows how you're going to carry out testing. It is, if you like, the design specification for your testing. Writing a test strategy will make you to think about how you're going to test the product(s) produced by your project.

It needn't be a big document but needs to show:-

- What you're going to test

- How you're going to test it

- Resources needed in terms of people, equipment and environments

- How long you're planning to take

Your test strategy checks will usually need to include:-

- System testing (does what's been built conform to the specified requirements?)

- Acceptance/user testing (does it work operationally?)

- Performance/stress testing (does it work under load and meet performance requirements?)

- Security testing (for example, are you sure that an IT system can't be breached or that a process isn't open to internal or telephone fraud?)

- Model Office Testing (simulating usage in a real working environment – usually this is only carried out in big or complex implementations, such as a call centre set-up where systems, telephony and processes are new and staff have been recruited and trained).

Having a clear test strategy is especially important when outsourcing work. In particular, you should always carry out your own acceptance/user testing where you've utilized outside resources, to test the quality of what's been delivered.

Inputs to this stage	• Requirements definition • Documented risks

Actions within this stage	• Design what needs to be delivered, e.g.
	
	   o IT solution design
	
	   o Business operational design including process changes
	
	   o Approach to training
	
	   o Approach to testing
	
	• Hold a meeting to review and sign off complete designs
	
	• Review and baseline estimates and plans in light of agreed design
	
	• Review risks in light of agreed design
	
	• Hold Project Board meeting at the end of this stage

Outputs from this stage	• Signed off Design Definition • Test Strategy • Updated risks • Baselined estimates and plan

Review estimates, plans, risks and issues

Just as at the requirements stage, estimates and plan need to be revisited when the detailed designs are complete, as seen on the chart on the previous page.

Again, it's not uncommon for costs to increase, given the detail added by the design.

It will be the responsibility of the Project Board to agree any increase in costs, or to ask the project manager to reduce scope.

If this cannot be done and the new costs exceed the benefits, the Project Board should consider whether the project needs to be stopped.

It's also a good idea to review the risks and issues at the end of the design stage. You may uncover new ones via detailed design work or, more positively, existing risks or issues may be resolved.

The team should, by now, have thought through how the project will be delivered, and will have a very good idea of what it's going to cost to complete it. Thus the estimates and plan should now present accurate costs and plans for completion of the project.

At the end of Design, estimates and plans are commonly referred to as 'baselined', meaning they are complete and show delivery dates that you're confident you can meet.

Project Board

Having completed another important part of the project, the Project Board should be reconvened to approve the final estimates and plans, and made aware of any new risks and issues that have manifested themselves.

Producing a design as a service company

Much of the time your designs will to have to fit in with other parts of a customer's existing infrastructure or standards, so you may want to invite relevant parties from their organization to your design review.

Needless to say, you should always make sure your customer agrees the design before going into production. Again, and depending on its complexity, you may decide to organize a walkthrough of its elements to make sure your customer has completely understood every facet.

At the expense of repetition, it's never a bad idea to make sure all 'i's are dotted and 't's crossed when it comes to sign-offs. Many a great relationship between customer and supplier has been ruined by misunderstandings.

Build

At last you can do the bit you'd been wanting to do before I made you do all that boring stuff!

The build stage is when you finally get to achieve what was specified in the Analysis and Design stages. Hooray! The specialists who designed the solution can now go ahead and build the product.

Inputs to this stage	• Signed off Design definition • Updated risks • Baselined estimates and plan
Actions within this stage	• Build deliverables, e.g. IT, processes, infrastructure, training, user guides • Document tests and expected results • Hold Project Board meeting at the end of the stage
Outputs from this stage	• Completed IT, processes, test scripts, training, user guides and any other elements of build, ready for testing

Although this is frequently the longest stage, assuming you've done all the aforementioned preparation it should also be the most straightforward one. It's what everyone's been champing at the bit to do since the project started!

However... in my experience the build part of the project is also the most likely to go over budget. It's an odd truism that people become most optimistic when estimating something they know a lot about – 'it sounds easy, it shouldn't take long' – so it's not uncommon for build estimates to be undercooked.

If you're building software it's a good idea to give your business/customers as early a view of any user interfaces as possible. This provides the opportunity for initial feedback and avoids issues later down the line, when they'll be more expensive to correct.

You might feel more secure doing this by building a one-off throwaway prototype, but usually you can show the real code, without the final validation and back-end software.

This also helps maintain links between developers and the business/customers, and encourages the collaborative approach that is essential for success in any project.

Document tests and expected results

As well as building the deliverables you'll need to develop tests to use during the Test stage, which comes next (see page 55).

These must be able to validate that the deliverables conform to the design specifications. Each test will consist of a description of the test (sometimes referred to as a 'test case') and the expected result of running it. Testing, as you'd expect, will allow you to confirm that the actual results match the expected results.

Tests need to be documented so that they can be reviewed for completeness, may be repeated, and can be used to justify the amount of effort required to run them.

You can write up tests in a document or spreadsheet, or use a testing tool (there's more information on these in the next section, Test).

Standards

To make it easier to support, it's important that what you build is developed to consistent standards. Processes, user guides and training will be far more usable if they are built to a uniform standard.

IT code should be built to set publishing standards, and lots of standards for programming languages are published on the internet.

If you're outsourcing work, talk to your supplier about development standards. Most will have their own standards or will be happy to work to ones that you supply.

Unit testing

Unit (or development) tests entail discrete elements of your product being tested in isolation. Only when a unit has passed all tests satisfactorily, with any faults rectified, should it go into a fully integrated system test alongside the rest of the product.

Fixing faults as early as possible saves time and re-working later in the process, so the Build stage should always include an element of ongoing testing as development continues. Do you really want to wait for the final system test to discover all the faults, rather than isolating and fixing them before they're harder to locate?

Test

Launching untested products can shatter your business, reputation and nerves

If you do nothing else well on your project, do the testing well.

You need to be 100% certain that the build stage has delivered what was specified in the Requirements and Design. If it doesn't – and depending on the severity of the faults and their implications to your customer and theirs - you might find yourself with a criminal record and huge debts, as well as egg on your face and a lost client.

"How many more times do I have to tell you? No more testing!"

Inputs to this stage	• Completed IT systems, processes, test scripts, training and any other elements of build, complete and ready for testing
Actions within this stage	• Carry out system testing to make sure that what has been built is what was specified
	• Test non-functional requirements, such as performance and resilience
	• Carry out user testing – does what was built work in a user scenario?
	• Carry out process walkthroughs
	• Deliver training
	• Develop the implementation plan
	• Hold a go/no-go meeting to approve readiness for go live
	• Hold a go/no-go Project Board meeting
Outputs from this stage	• All testing complete
	• Implementation plan
	• Go/no-go decision made

The most important stage

Get testing wrong and you potentially end up wrecking your productivity, your reputation, your legality or possibly all three. People tend to associate testing with IT, but an untested process can have disastrous results if opened up to the public.

It should go without saying that you should always formally walk through changed processes before implementing them. It should be as unthinkable as opening an untested road bridge or launching an untested plane.

You have to be exceptionally lucky for anything to work well on its first exposure to the real world, so going live without testing is a very risky strategy. Don't do it.

Be thorough

The other rule with testing is to be thorough; it should be obvious that there's little point in testing something unless you do it properly. The risks of cutting corners always outweighs the benefits and the costs of fixing something after go-live are much higher than they would have been earlier in the process.

That said, there's a difference between being thorough and being ridiculously over-cautious. There are reasonable limits to testing!

Phases of testing

Your test strategy (see page 47) should have decided how you're going to test, and you should anticipate covering some or all of the following phases:-

- System testing

- Acceptance/user testing

- Performance/stress testing

- Security testing

- Model office testing

Test automation

Testing of IT systems is, to an ever-increasing degree, carried out using automated test tools. With an automated test tool, you write the test once and can then run it many times.

Another advantage of automated tests is that they remain after you've delivered the system, so if you need to make changes later you'll be able to re-run the original tests to make sure that you haven't broken anything. This is commonly referred to as regression testing.

The number of test tools available is expanding rapidly. As I type, **QTP** by Hewlett Packard is the most widely used automation tool. **Selenium** is popular, free and can be used to automate the testing of browser-based software, while **Axe** from Odin and **eggPlant** from **TestPlant** are also capable tools with a significant following.

Outsourcing

If you're outsourcing any aspect of the project, don't trust the external company to do all the testing. You should always carry out final user/acceptance testing in-house, as a quality check on their work, and may find it advantageous to attach a stage payment to them successfully passing the acceptance test. It's a great incentive for them to work to a high standard, and without cutting corners.

Finding and fixing

You should maintain a fault log throughout testing, showing both open and closed faults, and noting their severity as well as what action is being taken to resolve them. A spreadsheet should be sufficient for this, but there are also bespoke software tools that will do it for you.

HP's **Quality Centre** is very popular, but isn't cheap. You might want to have a look at **Bugzilla**, which is free and widely used but lacks the professional support of paid for packages. The latter provides the functionality to allow you to manage all testing, so it's worth a look.

As testing progresses, particularly if you have a supplier involved or when the project is substantial, you may want to organize and run regular test review meetings, based around the fault log. I usually run these on a daily basis when I'm a few weeks away from the deadline to complete testing.

Testing as a service company

If you work in or run a service company you should go through the stages of testing described earlier. However, you can also expect your client to carry out final acceptance testing before agreeing that you've delivered what was required.

Agree what criteria will be applied to allow acceptance testing to be signed off as complete. If you don't, there's a danger that the customer will refuse to accept the finished product until all faults are removed, no matter how minor.

You will also, of course, need to provide support to acceptance testing and warranty support after the product is delivered.

Implementation plan

Developing an implementation plan can be very simple, when you're putting in place a new process, for instance; but very complex where, say, an IT change is made across a number of systems, requiring database updates and closure of a website while the change is implemented.

Such plans are usually structured by the hour rather than by the day or week. You might want to produce them using project planning software, but alternatively you can work from a list of tasks and timings on a spreadsheet.

Where systems implementation in particular is concerned, some measure of pre-go-live testing should be carried out in the production environment before final go-live. This isn't meant to repeat the testing you've already carried out, but is simply to ensure that systems have migrated correctly into the production environment.

Any implementation plan should contain a contingency plan or procedure in case something goes wrong and there's no time to fix it.

It should also include agreed escalation points so that, should something go wrong, the implementation team knows who to contact for a decision on whether they should back-out the system.

This is particularly important for IT implementations taking place out of office hours.

Go/no-go

Once all testing has passed to a level acceptable for go-live, you'll need to get permission from the Project Board to implement the change.

You don't have to be fault-free to go live (almost all IT systems go live with faults), but you do need to fix or find work-arounds for faults assessed as serious enough to cause problems post go-live. As importantly, you need to be able to convince the Project Board that the change is, in fact, ready to go live.

Be very careful about the number of work-arounds you agree to accept. If these accumulate as each new change is implemented, the odds are that you'll never have enough time to fix them properly. This builds up what's known as 'Technical Debt', where the cost of supporting work-arounds outweighs the advantages of making these compromises in the first place.

Training

If you need to deliver training it's carried out at this stage, so staff who need to use and support the change are trained just in time for go-live. In short, be prepared.

Implement

Don't fall at the final hurdle – plan what you need to do to make your go-live go without a hitch

Now for the scary bit – going live, when the implementation stage applies the changes into the real world. This can be as simple as flicking a switch or may be quite complex and take several hours, days or even weeks to complete. During the implementation stage, you'll be following the implementation plan you developed in the testing stage.

Inputs to this stage	<ul><li>All testing complete</li><li>Implementation plan</li><li>Go/no-go decision made</li></ul>
Actions within this stage	<ul><li>Move changes into production<ul><li>Move IT changes into production environments</li><li>Move business process changes into production</li></ul></li><li>Run warranty</li></ul>
Outputs from this stage	<ul><li>Implementation report issued</li><li>Warranty complete</li></ul>

Warranty

Make sure a warranty is included with anything delivered by a supplier. This should last for at least a month but could be much longer, depending on what you are buying.

Warranties don't just apply to hardware and software but can help to ensure that the team who built the change will still be available if something goes wrong.

Unless you're buying an off-the-shelf product with no modifications, push for the warranty to be provided by the supplier's development team, where relevant, not their Product Support team. The latter is unlikely to be fully conversant with the changes made for you.

It's a good idea to hold daily meetings with all appropriate personnel immediately following go-live, to monitor any post go-live issues and act to remedy them quickly. As the change settles down, you can meet less frequently.

Roll out

An implementation can take weeks where a roll out to a number of sites is involved. It could include computer hardware installation, software distribution, and/or the roll out of new processes and training. In this situation you would expect to put together a roll-out plan as part of implementation planning.

Implementation report

Depending on how complex your change is, the report might be an email, or a small document confirming that the change has been successfully implemented and that the warranty is in place.

Closure

I want to move on to the next project – now! Great, but first close this one properly...

It doesn't take long to tidy everything up. What's more, you're likely to find baring your soul in a 'lessons learned' session a surprisingly rewarding experience.

The objective of the Closure stage is to ensure that the business case is reviewed, new or increased organizational risks arising from the project are managed going forward, and lessons are learned from the whole experience.

Inputs to this stage	• Implementation report issued • Warranty complete
Actions within this stage	• Hold final Project Board meeting to review actual benefits and costs • Hand over outstanding risks to operational departments • Produce closure report including lessons learned
Outputs from this stage	• Signed off project closure report

It's very easy to skip this stage, given that the project is complete, and there's usually another project waiting in the wings. But try to make sure you close each project properly and, in particular, meet to discuss what could have been done better. It's so important to capture lessons learned, to avoid making the same mistakes next time.

Lessons Learned

Project teams, rather surprisingly, seem to love laying bare all of their mistakes (and especially the project manager's mistakes!) at the end of a project. These can be very instructive and enjoyable meetings.

One other piece of advice with lessons learned is to make sure that the learning is actually taken on board. It's depressingly common to find that the benefits of experience and hindsight are forgotten by the time the next project comes along.

The airline industry's a shining example of how learning lessons – and applying them – can make an amazing difference. In 1978, the number of aircraft accidents per million departures stood at thirty. Today it's fewer than five.

Each accident is poured over by investigators, anxious to avoid a repetition. Okay, the outcome of your projects may not be a matter of life and death, but think how *your* business could take off if you can achieve this level of improvement. Go for it!

Agile v Waterfall

Agile's philosophy is spot on, so if you're doing an IT project you may want to give it a go – or not

The delivery methodology described so far in this book is commonly known as **Waterfall.** It relies, as its name implies, on completed requirements cascading into your design; completed design cascading into the build; and finally, the build flowing into the testing at the end. It's all good, tried and tested stuff that takes you through your project in a logical, vertical sequence of events.

However, many top project managers have being using it for years, and it's hard to escape the buzz around **Agile** right now.

Don't know what it is? Let me help. Essentially, Agile is a variation on how to run and deliver a project. It's mainly used in and attuned to the needs of IT developments, although the principles could be applied to many other types of project.

The basic principle of Agile is to encourage developers and customers to work together from the start. So instead of generating a design, then building it, and then testing it, you'll work in short iterations.

Slice by slice, functionality is designed, built and tested by a unified team of developers and business/customers and, if possible, released into production.

This means analysts, developers, testers and customers have to collaborate at each stage, working closely together and preferably, in close physical proximity to one another. It also emphasizes the empowerment of development teams to self-organize and take responsibility for their work.

However, this leads to new challenges, because with Waterfall, everyone's committed to working towards and delivering a set number of requirements within a set timeframe.

Agile acknowledges that this is difficult to achieve at the best of times; people miss things in their reviews of design specifications, change their minds or, indeed, the world may change while the project is being developed.

This methodology offers a handy form of 'design as you go', if you like, as an alternative to the litany of change requests you may be asked to make to a baselined document.

What's baselined in an Agile project is the timescale. In effect, teams have to deliver as many of the requirements as they can within a given timeframe. If, by this deadline, there isn't enough functionality to satisfy the Project Board, a change request is raised to either extend the timeframe or to modify requirements.

However, the decision to move to a radically different system shouldn't be taken lightly, because it's far more than an alternative way of developing products. It necessitates a degree of reorganization throughout your company if you want to make it work.

Also be aware that it's rare for an entire system to be delivered exclusively by Agile, so quite often projects use a mixture of Agile and Waterfall for optimum results.

Agile positives

- More flexible

- Designed to be collaborative, so should bring developers, testers, analysts and customers much closer together, increasing the chances of delivering a better product

- Communicative by nature

- Incremental – so allows you to show tangible deliverables earlier and release what you've got, rather than waiting for full functionality to arrive.

Agile negatives

- Requires significant organizational change and commitment from senior management to make it work

- Business/customer staff on the project, who have other jobs to do, may find it hard work

- It depends on the application as to whether it's actually possible to deliver incrementally into production – you may still need to get to the end before you can go live

- Start and end points may look quite different from expectations because of Agile's flexibility to change. This may not work well for all customers and can cause issues with other departments, for example a marketing department trying to promote a revised product

- Tends to put much more dependency on having a very capable project team.

Waterfall positives

- Clearly defined start and end points

- Can be a lot easier for busy business/customer staff with other commitments

- You get what you ask for, which resonates well with the way many budget-holders like to work, i.e. give me a defined scope, within a defined timescale, for a defined cost.

Waterfall negatives:

- Much less flexible to change once the project is underway

- Can be less collaborative and communicative (dependent on how well the project is managed)

- A stronger tendency to demarcate business/users from developers.

Which should you choose?

Both camps have their supporters but the computer industry – with its usual ability to sell anything new as the answer to life, the universe and everything – is busily selling Agile with huge enthusiasm.

However, it's important to take on board that despite it receiving a much better press than Waterfall right now, both methodologies have resulted in some spectacular project failures. Don't get carried away with the notion that Agile will be quicker and cheaper and solve all your problems, because there are no guarantees and you're only as good as your team.

However, it's true that it may develop better software for you because of the way it encourages collaboration and continual improvement. If you decide to try it, to have any chance of success it's vital that you provide specific training for all staff who will be involved in the project, including the Project Board. You should also make sure that you have full buy-in from senior management.

You don't have to take my word for it. Recent research by VersionOne listed the top causes of failure in Agile projects as: lack of experience with Agile methods (44%), company culture/philosophy at odds with Agile (42%) and lack of management support (38%). You have been warned.

One danger with an Agile approach is that it's used as an excuse to throw most of the preparation out of the window and just get on with development. That isn't its intention or purpose, and would be a distortion of the approach. Additionally, you may have heard that Waterfall is all about command and control while Agile is associated with empowerment and delegation. Trust me: it's a myth.

Project managers who work by command and control are, in my opinion, destined to fail whatever they use; and while Agile does make it harder for individuals to impose their iron will on others, it doesn't render it impossible.

Likewise, the Agile principles – of keeping it small, giving the people doing the work responsibility for it and communicating well – aren't the sole preserve of their brand. Good project managers do all those things regardless of the methodology used.

Essentially, Waterfall tends to be best suited to projects and organizations that have a clear picture of the final product and don't believe they'll need to vary it during the project. Agile provides much greater flexibility to change, but offers less certainty about the end result and the delivery date.

Flavors of Agile

There are several Agile 'flavors', or methodologies, such as DSDM, Scrum and Extreme Programming. Of these, **Scrum** seems to have gained most traction and is the variant I'll describe here.

While Scrum isn't complex or difficult to understand, teams adopting it will have lots of questions. I strongly recommend that you run a training course for all prospective members of the team – including senior management – if you're considering trialing or using it.

A move to Scrum will result in organizational change for everyone involved, and won't merely be 'something new that the programmers are trying out'. It probably won't be easy to start with, but will become far less challenging as you all become familiar with it, and used to how it works.

There are some excellent books dedicated to Scrum, which go into more detail, but the following descriptions will give you a pretty good idea of the concept.

Key roles

The *Scrum Master*

This person must understand the rules of Scrum clearly, and is responsible for ensuring that the rules are followed. He or she facilitates meetings, provides some leadership and supports the team, but does not fulfil a management role in the Scrum team. This is because one of Scrum's defining principles is that development teams should be self-managing.

The *Product Owner*

Responsible for managing the Product Backlog, the Product Owner is ultimately accountable for what is delivered. Whoever fulfils this role is effectively the functional authority for the product being created. This entails agreeing the requirements in the Product Backlog, and taking responsibility for setting priorities and accepting the completed deliverables.

Scrum Lifecycle

Let's move on to the basic lifecycle, step by step:-

Product Backlog

The Scrum lifecycle begins with the capture of requirements in a pretty similar way to that described on page 39, so it might be worth flicking back a few pages to refresh your memory. Bear in mind that in Scrum, requirements are referred to as the Product Backlog and should, ideally, be one-liners expressed as user stories.

The Product Backlog is still owned, unsurprisingly, by the Product Owner, who will have overall responsibility for the end product being made. Typically this is the same person who would own and sign off the requirements using Waterfall.

A Product Backlog will still contain an indication of priorities, which will affect the order in which requirements are implemented. It may also contain acceptance criteria for each requirement, which will give the project team an indication of how they should test that function.

Sprints

The project will deliver in Sprints. These are time slots of a defined length, during which the development team will deliver functionality. Ideally, each Sprint should be capable of delivering something discrete, that can be put into production, though this isn't always possible.

At the start of a project, the development team will estimate, in order of priority, how long each requirement in the Product Backlog will take to deliver.

The best Sprint length is then determined, set to a duration that they think is needed to deliver something meaningful. Every Sprint on the project will be the same length.

A Sprint can be as short as a single week, but more typically will be four weeks long. If it doesn't prove possible to fit all planned requirements into the allotted duration, undelivered ones will be carried forward to the next Sprint.

Sprint Zero

Sprint Zero is the name given to the start-up phase – similar to that described on page 31 – when preparation for the Scrum project takes place.

Meetings (or just one, for a smaller project) are held to agree standards and procedures and to ensure that everyone understands the product, the project and how it's going to work.

Typically, Sprint Zero is very short, lasting one or two weeks. Uniquely, this phase doesn't have to be the same length as the other sprints; it's the only exception to the rule.

Agile shouldn't be viewed as an excuse to dispense with all documentation. Designs will still need to be thought out and documented, testers will still need to produce and run test scripts and support teams will still need to maintain the software, so it's essential that proper disciplines are maintained.

Sprints 1-n

The remaining Sprints are where the code is designed and written (assuming you're working on an IT project) and testing is carried out.

While there will usually have been some initial work to propose how functionality in the Product Backlog should be fitted into Sprints, the actual content of each one will be determined by Sprint Planning. This, then, is the first activity to be carried out in each Sprint.

Sprint planning

Sprint planning is carried out by the whole Sprint team and is time-boxed to a maximum of eight hours for a four-week Sprint, and proportionately less for shorter duration Sprints.

When planning, the team needs to be clear about what resources and personnel will be available and, in the case of the latter, how much time they can devote to the development of the Sprint.

At the start of this stage, the Sprint team, step by step and in order of priority, will select the **requirements** they believe can be completed in the time allotted for the Sprint, and transfer them from the Product Backlog to the Sprint Backlog.

They then add all **tasks** that must be completed to build those requirements into the Sprint Backlog and, after that, assign **time estimates and owners** to each of them.

Hence the Backlog effectively becomes a plan that will be updated as it becomes clearer what work is required or remains to be done.

As each Sprint completes, the Sprint Team must try to understand its velocity (in terms of speed and productivity) with a view to re-assessing how quickly requirements can be implemented, and should then apply this information to planning the next Sprint. In this way, they continually improve estimates and plans.

To further clarify what's being done when, and to understand dependencies, they may also decide to produce a visual, integrated plan for the Sprint, using a project planning tool, spreadsheet or even a hand-drawn plan. Given the relatively short timeframe, these planning tools don't need to be very sophisticated. Once planning is complete, work can begin.

Sprint Backlog

The Sprint Backlog, usually in the form of a spreadsheet, will include the requirements to be implemented in the current Sprint, the tasks that need to be completed for each requirement; a list of who is responsible for each task; the status of each task; an overall estimate of the work to be done; and any work remaining for each task.

It's common, in Agile, to use this spreadsheet to produce a burndown chart, which is a graphical representation of the *planned* rate of progress against the *actual* rate of progress. If all tasks aren't satisfactorily achieved by the end of the Sprint, it's clear that the velocity was slower than assumed, so the next Sprint can be adjusted accordingly.

Daily Scrum Meetings

The daily meeting, in my opinion, is one of the best features of Agile. It's attended by the whole Sprint team to monitor progress, raise issues and gain any required clarifications from the Product Owner.

Meetings are theoretically time-boxed to fifteen minutes (you may find that in practical terms it takes a little longer, but they certainly should be capped at no more than half an hour).

They're often described as stand-up meetings because attendees are encouraged to remain on their feet rather than sitting down, getting nice and comfortable and taking their time!

Ideally each member of the development team should explain:

- What they did yesterday

- What they will do today

- Any impediments they see that may prevent them or the team from progressing

Updates by each Sprint team member regarding the anticipated time remaining to complete his or her tasks within the Sprint, should be given at this meeting or to the Scrum Master. This data can then be incorporated into the Sprint Backlog.

Sprint Review

A Sprint Review is held at the end of each Sprint, and involves all members of the Sprint team. Its purpose is to agree what has been completed with the Product Owner and may therefore be accepted as ready for production.

Again, this meeting is time-boxed: four hours for a four-week Sprint and proportionately less for a shorter Sprint. Given that the team will have been meeting daily to assess progress, there shouldn't be any surprises and it should go smoothly. However, if functions cannot be accepted as completed, this meeting will agree to move them into the next Sprint.

Sprints will continue until such time as either the entire Product Backlog has been implemented, or the Product Owner, Project Manager and Project Board agree that sufficient functionality has been implemented.

Sprint Retrospective

This is the name for the final meeting held for each Sprint and is a smaller version of the Lessons Learned meeting (see page 64).

It gives the team an opportunity to discuss and evaluate what went well and what didn't, and to re-examine velocity. Of course this data is gathered with a view to using it to improve estimates, planning and performance during the next and subsequent Sprints.

If it's been agreed that you'll move code from this Sprint into production, it can be done by staff outside the original team. If so, the planning meeting for the next Sprint will need to allow for this, since the support that's likely to be required (at and after go-live) may affect the availability of resources.

Using Scrum as a service company

Scrum can be difficult for a service company. It's not as simple as agreeing a detailed specification to a price and timescale, and then getting on with it and delivering. You need to prepare for a lot more involvement from your customer than with a Waterfall project.

This means it's important that your client understands how Scrum works, and is happy and enthusiastic about working collaboratively. To hit a fixed timeframe and price you'll still want to fix some element of the project; and given you can't tie down the detailed functionality, the obvious parameter to fix is the number of Sprints.

Given the inherent flexibility of Scrum, you have to make sure – 100% sure – that your customer understands that it may not be possible to implement all requirements within the quoted timescales. This means careful prioritizing is essential, so that key deliverables are produced.

You also need to be aware of the velocity you're achieving as you work though each Sprint, and try to maintain a clear overview so that you understand how it will affect the overall project. If requirements have to be pushed into the next Sprint, again it's important to grasp the likely effect on the whole project.

Part of your Sprint Review should include working out what can be done to bring the project back on track if it looks as though things might slip. The team needs to be trained to use a combination of creative thinking and prioritization to try to find solutions.

A typical Scrum project

It's likely that most organizations will run projects that combine some elements of Scrum and some of Waterfall. Here, as an example, is a project that successfully delivered a new savings product for a bank, and demanded that a number of pieces of work were completed:-

1. Web and back office front ends. Agile was ideal for this, and Scrum was used

2. Changes to the back-end banking system. This was outsourced to an external company and because of the way the system was constructed and the company worked, Scrum was not deemed suitable. A Waterfall approach was used

3. Process changes. Again, not seen as suitable for a Scrum approach, but the process change team attended many Scrum Team meetings to allow it to keep close to what was being developed

4. Customer journey/marketing. Again, given the nature of the work and the degree to which it was outsourced, it was developed outside the Scrum paradigm.

The overall project was managed as follows:-

- Business case and start-up managed exactly as seen on pages 13 and 31. Estimates arrived at for all elements of delivery, including those to be carried out using Scrum and those not

- Analysis carried out as on page 39, except that front-end functionality was expressed in the form of a Product Backlog rather than traditional requirements

- Design, build and test carried out traditionally for everything except front ends, which were developed using Scrum

- Integration test and user acceptance test undertaken for whole system, including front and back ends and processes (in the case of acceptance test).

- Implementation and warranty carried out as shown on page 63

- The project manager managed the overall project, attending daily Scrum meetings mainly as an observer.

- Weekly project meetings were held in addition to the daily Scrum meetings.

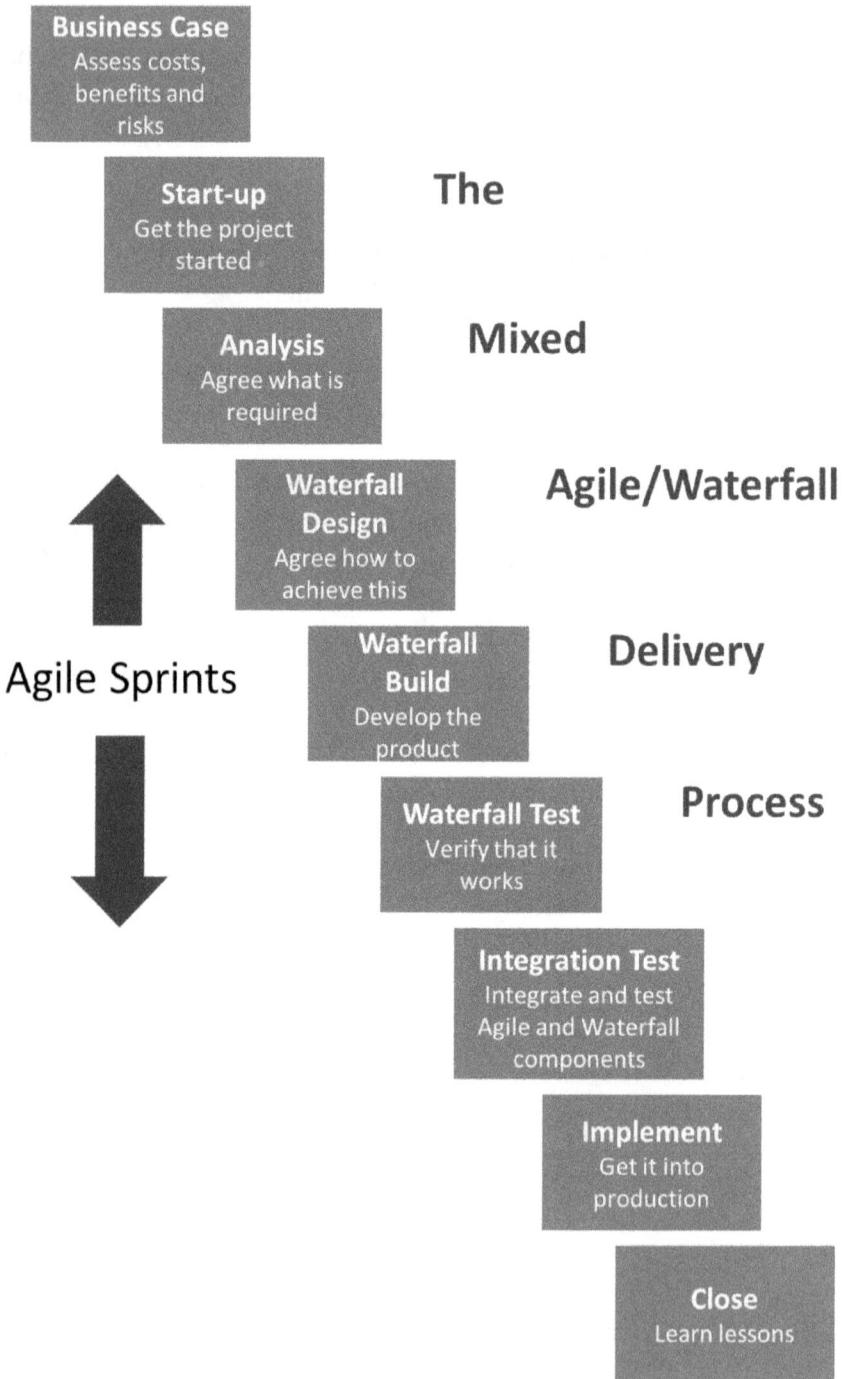

Business Case
Assess costs, benefits and risks

Start-up
Get the project started

The

Analysis
Agree what is required

Mixed

Waterfall Design
Agree how to achieve this

Agile/Waterfall

Agile Sprints

Waterfall Build
Develop the product

Delivery

Waterfall Test
Verify that it works

Process

Integration Test
Integrate and test Agile and Waterfall components

Implement
Get it into production

Close
Learn lessons

3

PROJECT GOVERNANCE

Governance

It may sound boring, but it's at the very heart of making your projects work

The importance of good governance

Governance has a bit of a worthy sound to it and perhaps, as a result, many small businesses fail to understand its importance or are simply scared away.

That's a shame. You can put some great processes and highly trained project managers in place but in the absence of good governance, you may as well not bother.

Successful project delivery starts at the top. If the company's Board isn't fully committed to project delivery, you're going to have problems. They should also take a strong interest in the progress and success of projects via the Project Sponsors, most of whom will probably be Board members.

The Project Sponsor and Project Board are there to both challenge and support the Project Manager from the very start to the very end. While providing genuine support from day one to delivery, the Board should be prepared to keep the Project Manager on the ball by asking difficult questions when appropriate.

Documentation deliverables

Don't be daunted by documents and records. They're designed to ease your life, not complicate it, by keeping you organized and in control, with all relevant facts, figures and plans to hand.

The basic set of documents found on the next few pages is likely to be all you'll need to manage a successful project. A suggested layout for each one is shown at the end of the book.

It's a good idea to set your documents up as templates. They will then act as a training aid for anyone new to the process, saving you from reinventing the wheel each time you run a project, encouraging consistency and generally speeding things up.

If you want to save even more time and effort, you can buy ready-made templates, which also include lots of useful tips, from **PMresults.co.uk**

Project Control Documentation

Document	Description
Business Case	Describes the justification for carrying out the project, describing benefits, costs and risks
Project Initiation Document	Describes how the project will be run
Project Plan	Usually a Gantt chart, showing how activities in the project will be scheduled and who will carry out each activity
RAID log	Risk, assumptions, issues and dependencies log

Minuted project team meetings	These need only be in the form of emails, but it's important to keep a track of the decisions made in project meetings. Note that you could also use an action log to achieve this
Action log	A good idea – update after each project team meeting to show what actions have been agreed and who is responsible for them
Minuted supplier meetings	Very important to take minutes of meetings with suppliers. In disagreements or contractual disputes these may be used as legal documents
Project status reports	Usually monthly, showing project progress, tracking major risks and issues and showing performance against budget
Financial forecasting/ management	Spreadsheets tracking project spend against budget
Project closure report	Mainly lessons learned from the project
Project Board pack and minutes	Usually slides that update the project board on progress, risks and issues
Change request	An application to change the scope of the project

Design, Test and Implementation Documentation

Document	Description
Requirements definition/Product Backlog	Describes **what** is to be built
Design definition	Describes **how** project is to be built
Sprint Backlog	Describes the work to be carried out in a Sprint and its estimates to complete
Test strategy	Shows how testing will be organized and who is responsible for what
System test scripts and results	What you are going to test as well as expected and then actual results
User acceptance test scripts and results	What acceptance tests you are going to run as well as the expected and actual results
Go/no-go document	Confirms that the project is ready for implementation
Implementation plan	Shows how implementation will be carried out

Governance roles and responsibilities

Name of Role	Responsibility
Project Sponsor	The key role in the delivery of successful projects. Ultimately responsible for the project, supported by the Senior Supplier and Senior User. Ensures the project is focused on achieving its objectives
Senior Supplier/Product Owner	Represents the interests of those designing, developing, facilitating, procuring and implementing the project's products.
Senior User	Represents the interests of all those who will be using the project's products.
Project Manager	Has the authority to run the project on a day-to-day basis on behalf of the Project Board. Main responsibility is to ensure the project produces the required products on time, to budget and of the required quality.

Project reporting

Project reports are usually produced at two levels:

- A Project Status report informs on project progress, risks, issues and spend against budget – normally monthly

- A Project Board report informs the Project Board of much the same things at each Board meeting.

Project reports communicate progress to the team and Project Board, and are good discipline for the Project Manager.

They prompt him or her to check that progress they forecast the previous month has been achieved, and that risks and issues flagged up have been (or are being) resolved.

Having to present project finances also ensures that the project manager can explain any variance against budget.

Try to keep your reports short and to the point. If you want them to be read, don't over-elaborate; just get the important stuff across in as few words as you can. Bear in mind that what might entertain you or make you proud could send your audience to sleep!

A project is defined by its 'RAG' status, which is identified by assessing the agreed plan against three parameters: time, cost and quality.

One of three colours – red, amber or green – is selected to indicate the level of confidence as follows:

Red Status - the project will not deliver to the previously agreed plan/ budget/quality. The status can be corrected by the approval of a new plan (with revised timelines, budget and/or scope) by the Project Board.

Amber Status - there is a significant risk to the project, as the approved plan/budget/quality may not be achievable. As above, approval of a new plan can change the status.

Green Status - the project is progressing to the agreed plan, budget, quality and scope.

A **Project Status Report** should include:

- Date and project name

- RAG status

- Progress achieved this reporting period

- Progress expected next reporting period

- A list of milestones and their statuses

- Key issues

- Key risks

- Costs – actual against forecast spend.

A **Project Board Report** will be similar:

- Date and project name

- RAG Status

- Status in words – 2 or 3 bullets only

- High-level plan showing progress

- Costs – actual against forecast spend

- Key issues

- Key risks

- Items for decision at this board.

Project Board meetings

The Project Board will be chaired by the Project Sponsor, and meetings should be held at regular intervals during each project, ideally at the beginning and end of each stage.

The Project Manager must report project progress as well as highlighting major risks and issues at the Project Board meeting. The Project Board should offer help and support if any issues require escalation.

It's important that Project Board meetings are properly minuted in case there are queries at a later stage.

Project team meetings

Don't fall into the trap of communicating mostly by email, or by sending updates from a collaboration tool. Nothing beats face-to-face meetings for understanding progress, disseminating information, addressing issues and building team spirit.

Depending on the size of the project, project team meetings should be held weekly, even if this entails some members of the team attending by audio or video conference. Project team meetings will have a set agenda and review:

- Progress against the plan

- Actions due

- Risks and issues that are scheduled for action.

This is the Project Manager's opportunity to see how the project is tracking against plan and document outstanding actions using an action log. Be wary of tasks that are perpetually 'nearly' complete; if you're constantly told that a task is two days from completion, take action. Question the person involved to try to get to the bottom of the issue.

Supplier meetings

Depending on the way the project's organized, suppliers may attend project team meetings, or instead have separate meetings with the project manager. It's better if your supplier's project managers can attend your company's project team meetings, since all issues and views on progress and can then be aired at once, with everyone present.

Be aware that confidentiality or sensitive commercial issues may make it impossible to involve suppliers in all discussions at your team meetings, so you may occasionally have to leave these to the end, or ask them to step out for a while.

Separate governance meetings should be scheduled with the supplier, which their project manager and account manager can attend to review the project's progress and the quality of the supply.

I know I've said this time and time again but don't forget, especially when you're holding frequent or brief meetings, that all of them need to be minuted. In any dispute these minutes will become contractually important documents, and you'll forgive the repetition.

Risk and Issue Management

Feel free to ignore this section if you're a free spirit who doesn't mind nasty surprises

I'm no gambler, but tell me you don't manage risks and I'll be happy to stick my neck out and wager that your project will be full of 'em.

The point of the managing risk is to try to understand what might go wrong on a project so that you can make adequate preparations, should the worst happen. If you don't manage risks you'll just be reacting to events as they occur. It'll be unpredictable, stressful for everyone concerned, and more likely to lead to delays or increased costs.

All projects have risks of one sort or another and it's very important to both identify and manage them.

"Let's try it without the parachute"

Risk Reviews

You need to fully assess the threats to each new project, and this is most effectively done by holding a formal Risk Review, where key members of the project team are brought together. At this meeting you'll cover what risks are present, the likelihood of these occurring and the outcomes if they do. You can also agree mitigations to lessen either the probability of an event occurring, or its impact if it does.

There are a number of ways of running it. The best approach is to ask for submissions of risks beforehand, and then review what's been submitted when you meet. If you're in an environment where it's difficult to get people to submit risks in advance, a 'post-it note session' or similar – where people come up with risks on the day and the project manager instigates discussions about them – can also work well.

Once you've gathered your risks they should be annotated in the RAID log (Risk, Assumptions, Issues and Dependencies) with review dates, and reviewed at project meetings when those dates come due. The focus of your review of risks should be on carrying out actions to resolve or mitigate them, and thus to prevent risks from becoming issues.

Beware of falling into the mindset that says managing and tracking risks is just 'admin'; and at the same time, don't go over the top.

Some risks are obvious and will be there for all projects – it's fine to put forward a risk that says 'If you don't get resource X by date Y then the project could slip', but non-specific risks such as 'If the project doesn't get any of its resources, it will slip', are givens, and everyone understands them already.

If you log too many generic and obvious risks you'll find it hard to see the wood for the trees and, worse, may end up overlooking an important potential threat.

Project status reports and Project Board packs should include your top five risks – those with the highest likelihood and highest impact – as well as a count of the number of significant risks, with high or medium likelihood and impact. The number of significant risks a project is carrying is generally a good indicator of its health.

If nothing is happening to resolve a significant risk, despite your and your team's efforts, you will need to escalate it to the Project Board.

Using the RAID Log to record risks

For any perceived risk, the log should include:

- A description of the risk

- The date that the risk was raised

- The likelihood of the risk becoming an issue

- The impact of the risk becoming an issue

- Proposed actions to mitigate the risk and who owns these

- A review date

Likelihood

Risks should be assessed according to the likelihood of the risk becoming an issue. A suggested scale for each risk is:

Probability	Low	Medium	High
Likelihood	0-25%	25%-50%	50%+

Impact

The impact of the risk becoming an issue is measured on budget or timescales. A suggested scale is:

Impact	Low	Medium	High
Budget increase	2%	10%	20%
Timescale increase	Less than 1 day	Less than 2 weeks	More than 2 weeks

Issues

While a 'risk' is something that could happen, an 'issue' is something that's already happened and needs immediate attention. Issues should be noted in the RAID Log and reviewed at frequent intervals until they cease to be issues. The log should include:

- A description of the issue

- The date the issue was raised

- The impact of the issue – as high, medium or low

- The status of the issue – as red, amber or green

- Actions to resolve the issue

- The owner of these actions

- A review date.

Change Control

What would happen if you asked someone to build a garage and then, once he'd started, requested a house?

Let's face it: change control is just common sense. You'd expect costs and timescales to go through the roof in that scenario, so why should any other type of project be different?

Projects are about delivering a defined scope within a set timeframe and budget. Clearly, it's just about impossible to do this unless the scope is controlled. Scope creep – the gradual process of work expanding without being managed – can kill projects.

As Project Manager it's not your job to stop change, but you do have to make sure that, after it's approved, everyone understands the timescale and budgetary impacts. Your budget and plan, against a list of requirements, must be regarded as the baseline for the project and needs to be change-controlled.

A change should be raised on a change request form, which should present a mini business case for it that explains its benefits as well as costs. The Project Manager will need to ask all parties affected by the change to cost its impact so that it can be presented to the Project Sponsor. He or she will usually approve changes, with final ratification being given by the Project Board.

Big changes are usually easy to spot, while cumulative small changes can be harder to detect and can be very destructive. It's therefore essential to communicate the importance of change control to all team members and stakeholders.

Projects in small companies are particularly prone to scope creep. The Chief Executive Officer and the sales force constantly talk to customers and find out what competitors are doing, so there's a huge temptation for them to pop along to whoever's doing the work and ask if they can 'just' incorporate a few new features.

Left to their own devices, if your supplier gets a call from your CEO asking them to add something, they'll probably jump to it – more money coming in! – and the same is likely to apply to your in-house teams. As Project Manager, you need to be in control of this.

A large part of controlling change is communicating to all concerned that it needs to be properly assessed, because it costs money and may delay the project. The classic line is 'I've talked to Fred and he says it will only take five minutes to change that,' which may be right. But then Fred realizes that the tiny change affects something else too; oh, and he hadn't considered the testing impact of the change, either.

Despite what you may read, using Agile doesn't mean change control is abolished. All projects, Waterfall or otherwise, have to work within budgets, so while changes might be more about timescale and costs here (agreeing to more Sprints), they still need to be agreed and approved by the Project Board.

Never use a project's contingency to absorb change. Tempting though it may be, contingency is there to cover the risk of something that doesn't go to plan, not to fund change.

Quality

Review it, test it and have a far happier life – how's that for an offer you can't refuse?

Quality control in projects is much misunderstood. People tend to associate quality with particular methods, when they should really be focusing on results.

A 'quality' deliverable is one that's fit for the purpose specified by the customer. A quality toaster for the home is likely to be completely different to one for a hotel, because of the volume of use each endures. Producing a domestic toaster to catering appliance standards is likely to result in a large and very expensive toaster with few benefits for the home user; do it the other way around and the hotel will end up with cheap toasters that soon break down.

The two major elements of quality control are:

- Review and sign off

- Testing

Review and sign off

A review is the single most effective means of maintaining quality.

It also provides a forum to encourage creativity and ideas: 'That's good, but have you thought about doing it this way instead.' Creative thinking comes more easily from groups than individuals. One person's idea can spark off a new, even more exciting thought in someone else.

So let your hair down. Review IT code, documents and processes – in fact, review everything you think you have completed. It isn't just a useful exercise but a cost-effective one. Devoting a relatively short time to a review removes errors early on and reduces the need for expensive re-working later.

All major requirements, deliverables and designs should be reviewed and signed off by the Senior User/Product Owner or someone they've delegated to do it in their absence. This ensures that there are no arguments down the line about exactly what was required.

Consider how you carry out reviews. Although it's become the norm to send documents by email, it's more involving and interactive to get interested parties together at a meeting to review the document.

It isn't hard to organize. All you'll need is:

- A chairperson

- A scribe to document agreed actions

- The author(s)

- Reviewers, including whoever's responsible for signing off.

Remember to instruct attendees to read the relevant document(s) before the review, and to come armed with their comments.

Testing

I'll keep it simple: test your deliverables properly. It's far more expensive to repair or change something after it's been delivered than it is to get it right first time.

Portfolio Management

With a project office function you'll stay in control, rather than making decisions on priorities on the hoof

'Project Office' conjures up an image of a large team of people in a big company, all carefully monitoring plans, counting project costs, monitoring risks and issues and generally keeping an eye on the project management team. What relevance can this possibly have to small and medium companies?

Team spirit goes a long way and makes a business greater than the sum of its parts. And it's true that – if your organization's small enough for everyone to muck in, talk to other employees and generally make things happen – you can sometimes hold a project together with chewing gum and string.

But if you're building a portfolio of projects to manage and you're starting to grow beyond small and veering towards medium, you should think about establishing a Project Office discipline. Whether you're developing products or providing services, once you start expanding, that brave team spirit often dissipates along with informal meetings in the coffee area, and making the team work effectively needs a lot more thought.

Lack of organization leads to money being wasted and chips away at morale, so it's important to get this right.

If you don't introduce a portfolio management function when a smaller company starts to grow, there's a danger that decisions about project initiatives and priorities will be uninformed; the consequence of this can be a seriously debilitating effect on both company growth and staff morale. So what are the key actions of a Project Office function in this scenario? Let's go through them one by one.

Strategy

All companies need an overall strategy.

It isn't the Project Office's job to provide this, but they'll be the ones who remind management to make decisions about which product developments to prioritize or what markets to sell services into; and that's a whole lot easier if the company has a clear strategy. Otherwise you'll be making decisions on the hoof, and getting dragged in all directions according to the flavour of the month.

The simplest way to devise the best strategy for your organization is to carry out a SWOT analysis (Strengths, Weaknesses, Opportunities and Threats). 'What do we do well?', 'What do we do badly?', 'Where do we want the company to go?', 'What are our competitors doing?'

Of course no strategy is set in stone, and it will need to be reviewed on at least an annual basis, but it's essential that you have one.

Build a project portfolio

There's often more demand for projects than can possibly be met, so the next thing you'll need is a project portfolio.

Get bids together from the various stakeholders in your company, measure their fit with strategy and do a brief assessment of costs and benefits for each of them. Senior managers will then need to meet to agree the portfolio's priority order, based on that information.

Manage your Portfolio

Once priorities are assigned, portfolio management by your Project Office function can:-

- Facilitate building full business cases for each project in the portfolio, showing detailed costs, benefits and risks for senior managers to consider/agree to proceed

- Capture time spent on each project to allow project managers to monitor actual costs against estimates

- Monitor resource usage to ensure that valuable staff are fully utilized, and help to resolve conflicts when staff are over-utilized

- Let senior management know the impact on the rest of the portfolio if there's a change in project priorities, a serious slippage in a project or a loss of a key member of staff.

In smaller companies, portfolio management is usually a function, not a huge department of project office staff. It's likely to be one member of staff, maybe doing it part-time.

However, it's best to introduce a proper portfolio management structure as soon as your company starts to grow. If you don't, there's a danger that decisions about project initiatives and priorities could become uninformed. The consequences can be a debilitating effect on both company growth and staff morale.

Be aware and plan ahead to avoid falling into this trap unwittingly.

4

SOFT SKILLS

Communication

'The single biggest problem in communication is the illusion that it has taken place'   *George Bernard Shaw*

There's no greater sin than boring your audience, so here's a simple rule for effective communication that will help you to avoid doing so: make what you say clear, concise and informative.

Communication is one of the most important parts of the Project Manager's job. You'll need to communicate with your team, with the Sponsor and members of the Project Board and with suppliers. In fact, it's been estimated that 70-90% of your time in this role will be spent communicating in one form or another.

Bear in mind that for some projects, communication is the only deliverable the stakeholders will actually see until the project is completed.

"Let's work on your communication style"

Meetings

We've all been to interminable meetings where we wished we'd been somewhere else. Many have found themselves fighting off drooping eyelids or – in the most embarrassing case scenario – waking up!

Meetings, like them or not, are a means of communicating and resolving issues, and may also be used for reviewing documents. If they're not your cup of tea, tough! They won't go away. They can, however, be made a lot more effective. There's little point in insisting that busy people attend meetings that waste their time, so follow these suggestions and you'll reduce the chances of it happening:

- Communicate the objectives and agenda to all participants before the meeting starts

- If a document is to be reviewed, brief participants to read it beforehand

- All appropriate people must be invited – and must attend

- Everyone should turn up on time

- The meeting owner needs to be prepared, and shouldn't just try to 'take it as it comes'

- He or she must keep the meeting to the agenda and avoid being side-tracked

- Numbers attending must be kept to the minimum required – don't invite spectators

- Actions and decisions from the meeting must be minuted and followed up.

You also need to decide how many meetings you, personally, need to attend. As Project Manager it's very easy to find yourself overwhelmed by them, so be selective. You don't need to go to them all, and need to trust team members to run meetings, and to find their own solutions to certain issues.

However, meetings are a good medium for you to collect data about the project. This might be hard data about progress against the plan, risks and issues, or useful information about how you think the team is working together, or concerns about a supplier.

Effective communication

Project managers can be swamped by emails; on big projects this can hit 150-200 a day, and it's inordinately time-consuming. You need to work out how to filter and prioritize them so you don't spend all day wading through irrelevant information. People will often copy you in because they think they should, or because they want to make sure you can't tell them you didn't know about something.

Don't think you have to fully read or respond to every one. After a while on a project, I find I can scan emails and filter them into:

- Junk – of no interest, move on
- Information – take note but leave it to whoever sent the email to sort out
- Action – need to respond
- Long email chain – stop now and get on the phone!

Some people like responding to emails as they arrive. I have to admit that I'm one of them, but you may find it better to allocate two or three times in the day to respond to your emails in batches.

I don't believe in communicating via protracted email chains, but it happens all the time. What could be sorted out in ten minutes, face-to-face or on the phone, turns into a long email thread, where everyone eventually loses track of what is going on.

Think before you click 'reply all' to an email. Does everyone on the email need to receive your reply? Are you just making other people's lives more difficult by copying them in on information about which they have little or no interest?

The best project managers communicate predominantly by speaking to people face-to-face, on the phone or by video conference. I've seen people trying to manage projects almost exclusively by email. Believe me, this is a really bad idea – get out there and talk to people!

Be concise, relevant and clear

Never forget that you're communicating with busy team members and staff. If you don't make your communications concise, clear and relevant to the people you send them to, you are wasting their time and yours.

Make sure you write in decent English (or whatever language you're using) and that you don't use fifty words where you could write ten. Personally, I never send an email without reading it through first. I'm astonished, at times, at the appalling English I've managed to produce at the first attempt!

When crafting your communications, imagine yourself in the recipients' shoes. An explanatory email containing intricate technical details might be appropriate for computer programmers, but a complete turn-off for a senior managers.

In other words – pun fully intended! – think about your reader/s and amend your language accordingly.

People Management

Persuade, charm, cajole, suggest and even plead, but please don't SHOUT at people or do their job!

Leadership

Clearly, project managers have to 'manage'. However process and governance, while absolutely essential, can be a little empty if you fail to demonstrate leadership, too.

Leadership is about looking at all of the available data, consulting with members of the team and Project Board and considering the impact on all stakeholders before making a decision.

All project managers need to make decisions. They may not always be decisions that the majority of the team agrees with, but a good leader will always be happy to explain the rationale for the decision.

Good leaders communicate and listen well, and encourage members of their team. Equally, leadership is about maintaining team spirit and morale, even when a project's experiencing problems.

Leaders develop trust. They show that they trust members of their team to deliver, and gain trust from their team and Project Board from the way they conduct the project – and themselves.

Micromanagement

Whether you're managing suppliers or in-house staff, it's important that you get your people skills right. If you don't you might as well add your name to topics for discussion at the Risk Review.

The clue is in the title: 'Project Manager'. It's about managing the project, not writing the requirements or designing it.

Too many project managers get overly involved in the technical side of a project and, as a result, get lost in the detail. Falling into this trap often means losing sight of the overall direction of the project, too, and additionally, can demotivate the staff whose job really *is* to sort out the technical aspects.

If you're living with a micromanagement fixation, go cold turkey and learn to delegate. Project managers who insist on getting involved in everything risk becoming less effective, partly because they're preventing themselves from seeing the bigger picture, and partly because the workload they generate for themselves means they simply burn out.

Delegate where you can and where appropriate. People in teams generally work better when they're given responsibility and know they're trusted to do the work. You need to ask questions and challenge, certainly, but you don't need to be hands-on.

Who's responsible for what should be clarified by the PID and further reinforced by the Project Plan. In larger projects, it's not uncommon to produce terms of reference so that people understand what they're expected to do, and the limits of their responsibilities.

Managing suppliers

Treat your suppliers well. You need the whole project team pulling together to help you deliver, and they're part of it. It'll do you no favours to treat suppliers poorly. You don't have to chastise a supplier every time they get something wrong. You've every right to expect them not to repeat mistakes, but they will make *some* initially. Be honest about your feelings about what's happened – and then move on.

I've witnessed very adversarial relationships develop with suppliers because the Project Manager has felt let down and, in an overcharged atmosphere, has become argumentative or angry. Keep your cool, because if your relationship with a supplier breaks down, the project has significantly less chance of delivering.

Persuasion, not aggression

There's a myth out there that project managers need to be aggressive, shout at people and bully a bit to get things delivered.

Nothing could be further from the truth, especially in small organizations, and where you have long-term relationships with both suppliers and employees.

There's little to be gained from upsetting people when you're trying to get a project delivered. The best in the business persuade and influence by bringing teams together and motivating them. This is rarely achieved by bullying.

I managed a huge system delivery for a Fortune Global 100 company. It was an 18-month project and, at the time, represented the largest implementation in their history. There was a massive amount of work to be done and the change touched so many of the company's systems that faults found after go-live would have had serious impacts.

Instead, the project delivered on time and budget and without any issues afterwards.

During a meeting with my line manager (an otherwise highly intelligent man), he congratulated me on the success of the project, but declared that a number of people couldn't understand how I'd done it. Some, apparently, were going as far as to suggest it must have been blind luck!

Feeling rather offended by this, after a year and a half of intense project management that had put all my skills and experience to the test, I asked why.

'You don't shout at people,' he said, 'and a lot of the senior staff can't believe anyone could deliver a project as big as this without shouting at people.'

Maybe I should bellow at the team now and again to enhance my reputation, he continued. I found it very disheartening to hear such views, but it's not an uncommon perception.

I've delivered a lot of projects and I'm proud to say that I've never had to shout at anyone to achieve this. A raised voice or eyebrow, perhaps. But yelling? Not once.

Persuade, cajole, plead, bribe, use diplomacy and pray (if that's your thing), but don't ever become aggressive. It may make you feel better, briefly, and provide a short-term gain, but it won't help deliver in the long run.

Setting objectives

Project-related individual objectives for key staff can be very good way of focusing them on the importance of delivering. Objectives can be reviewed annually, as part of their staff performance review.

It's surprising (or maybe it isn't!) how focused staff become when they think a financial incentive – perhaps a bonus or pay review – may be on the cards...

Crisis Management

Failure is inevitable at some stage – what you do when it happens is what counts

It's a well-used axiom that failure is a very important step on the road to success, and if someone tells you they've never failed they're either covering something up, or haven't done very much.

I've known people who have experienced multiple business failures before they learned from their mistakes, finally got the hang of it and went on to realize huge success. Even politicians have finally caught on to the notion that apologizing for a failure, rather than refusing to admit to having made a mistake, isn't such a bad idea.

Even the best-planned and managed projects can sometimes go wrong. People make mistakes and if they're big enough errors, this can create a crisis where timeframes and budgets go out of the window and it's all hands to the pumps to try to stabilize things.

So what should you do if you find yourself in this situation?

For a start, you need get some perspective. Take a mental step back. You're so close to it that you may feel as though it's the end of the world, but it's not the outbreak of nuclear war or famine. It's your project going wrong and it can – and will – get fixed.

At the point of crisis, with your project falling apart around you and all sorts of pressure being applied by senior managers and customers, the main thing you can learn to do is stay calm, considered and positive.

Stop worrying about whose fault it was and realize that, while it may only be temporary, your role has changed from Project Manager to

Crisis Manager. This has given you a chance to show how good you can be at managing your way out of one.

Too many people get dragged down by feelings of guilt and failure when something for which they're responsible goes horribly wrong. They fail to see the opportunity before them – a chance to shine as a hero or heroine who can take charge and move forward in a horribly stressful situation.

The chances are that to get to that situation, you and your team have made some mistakes. Accept it: everyone makes mistakes.

So don't spend time worrying about covering your backside or wallowing in misery. Instead, just say sorry – and then tell your team to be positive and explain that you want solutions, not excuses.

If you can start to recover the situation, you'll begin to feel better about yourself and can claw back lost pride and status. More than that, if you can get your team around you, in solid support, you can achieve remarkable things in a crisis.

This is often hard to appreciate when everything seems to be falling apart around you, but try to see failure at work as an opportunity, not a personal disaster.

Make sure that what people remember is the disaster that *nearly* happened but didn't, because – despite everything – the cool-headed Project Manager got it back on track.

5

AND FINALLY...

There's always an 'and finally'

Now for the tricky bit – it's time to go out and deliver those projects!

If you're raring to go, this book's done its job. So in conclusion, the key points you need to be aware of are:

- Work put in up front will pay dividends later. You can't build a house on mud – it needs proper foundations.

- Don't rush into a project. Put as much work as you can into understanding the initial scope and estimating costs and benefits

- Keep it small. Split big projects into manageable chunks.

- Review your estimates through the analysis and design stages. Costs usually go up, so make sure you have a strategy for this.

- Take the discovery and review of risks seriously; if you don't, you'll spend a lot of time reacting to issues that you could (and should) have anticipated and resolved earlier.

- Poor requirements cause many issues with projects – if you haven't resolved what you're trying to produce, you can't know whether you can deliver it on time and to budget.

- Don't ask suppliers for firm quotes until you've agreed your requirements or their costs will go up. If you introduce additional features later, they're going to cost more.

- Don't work in a silo. Projects are collaborative activities, where teamwork, sharing and communication are vital.

- Manage your stakeholders effectively – you're going to need their help and co-operation to deliver a project successfully.

- Your job isn't to stop change, but to control and cost it and make sure it is approved. Keep track of small, cumulative scope creeps that can derail a project, as well as the big changes.

- Don't skip documentation – it's there to make you think, and to communicate that thinking to others, not so you can point with pride at the mountains of paper you have produced.

- Quality is important – it's not an optional extra. It costs a lot less to get things right first time than to fix after you've delivered.

- Arrange reviews of requirements and designs throughout the project and make sure your testing is organized and thorough.

- Communication is very important, but make sure it's effective – don't become a slave to email, you need to talk to people!

- Be persuasive and diplomatic. Don't shout at people and don't fall out with your suppliers.

- Be positive and try to make the project an enjoyable experience for everyone. Your attitude and approach sets the tone for all members of the project team.

Document Layouts

"Almost all quality improvement comes via simplification of design, manufacturing... layout, processes, and procedures."
Tom Peters

On the next few pages you'll find typical layouts of the documents you are likely to use in the role of Project Manager, all of which have been explained earlier in this book. I hope they help.

Microsoft Word and Excel templates for these can be purchased at **PMresults.co.uk**

Business Case

Produced by	Project Manager
Use	To determine the justification for carrying out the project
Contents	Summary of scope Benefits Cost estimates Outline plan Major assumptions and dependencies Major risks
Usual format	PowerPoint slides
Signed off by	Senior management

Project Initiation Document (PID)

Produced by	Project Manager
Use	To describe how the project will be run
Contents	Project objectives
	Project scope and exclusions
	Project constraints and assumptions
	Project approach
	Summary of business case
	Project organization
	Quality plan
	Change control
	Initial Project Plan
	Risk management
	Communication
	Project filing structure
Usual format	Microsoft Word document
Signed off by	Project Board

Product Backlog/Requirements Definition

Produced by	Analyst in conjunction with Product Owner/Senior User
Use	To describe what is required to be built
Contents	Single line requirements or user stories Owner for each requirement Priority for each requirement
Usual format	Microsoft Excel spreadsheet
Signed off by	Product Owner/Senior User

Design Definition

Produced by	Technical experts in the areas being designed
Use	To describe how the requirements will be achieved
Contents	What is in scope What is out of scope Cross reference to requirements definition Solution design Impacts on other areas
Usual format	Microsoft Word document
Signed off by	Senior User, Project Manager, Build team

Sprint Backlog

Produced by	Development team
Use	To describe and plan the work to be carried out in each Sprint
Contents	Product Backlog item Sprint Backlog tasks Original estimates Planned burn down of days Actual burn down of days Burn down chart showing planned against actual
Usual format	Microsoft Excel document
Signed off by	Development Team

RAID Log (Risks, Assumptions, Issues and Dependencies)

Produced by	Project Manager and team
Use	To describe and monitor the risks, assumptions, issues and dependencies in the project
Contents	Risk description, date raised, raised by whom, likelihood and impact of risk, actions to mitigate risk, owner and review date.
	Assumption description, date raised, raised by whom, actions to verify assumption, owner and review date.
	Issue description, date raised, raised by whom, impact of issue, status of issue, actions to resolve issue, owner and review date.
	Dependency description, date raised, raised by whom, who the dependency is on, due date, impact of dependency, actions required, owner and review date.
Usual format	Microsoft Excel document
Signed off by	Project Manager

Project Plan

Produced by	Project Manager, but parts may be delegated to technical leads.
Use	To show the tasks to be completed by the project and progress in completing those tasks.
Contents	Typically a Gantt chart Tasks to be completed and who is responsible Dates Dependencies Deliverables
Usual format	Project planning tool
Signed off by	Project Board

Action Log

Produced by	Project Manager
Use	To annotate and track project actions
Contents	Action description Raised by Owner Due date Status Resolution
Usual format	Microsoft Excel document
Signed off by	n/a

Change Request

Produced by	Change proposer – could be any team member
Use	An application to change the scope of the project
Contents	Date raised and by whom
	Description of change
	Reason for change
	Business benefits if change implemented
	Business impact/risk if change not implemented
	Costs and impact of timescales
	Recommended action and authorization to proceed
Usual format	Microsoft Word document
Signed off by	Project Sponsor initially (for speed), final sign off by Project Board

Project Status Report

Produced by	Project Manager
Use	To show project status and progress
Contents	Reporting period RAG status Number of significant risks and issues What has been achieved this reporting period What is planned to be achieved next reporting period Progress against project milestones Key risks, issues and dependencies Change requests Budget forecasts against actuals
Usual format	Microsoft Word document
Signed off by	Senior management

Project Board Report

Produced by	Project Manager
Use	To update the project board on progress, risks and issues
Contents	Agenda Project status Outline plan, showing progress Costs, showing estimated against actual Key issues Key risks Key dependencies For decision by the Project Board (includes Change Requests)
Usual format	Microsoft PowerPoint document
Signed off by	Project Board

Test Strategy

Produced by	Test team
Use	To describe how testing will be organized and who will be responsible for what
Contents	What is in scope of testing What is out of scope of testing Description of planned testing • System testing • Acceptance testing • Regression testing • Performance testing • Security testing • Model Office testing
Usual format	Microsoft Word document
Signed off by	Project Manager and Senior User/Product Owner

Go/No-Go document

Produced by	Project Manager
Use	Confirms that the change is ready for implementation
Contents	Faults outstanding Systems – list affected systems and readiness for implementation Processes – list affected processes and readiness for implementation Regulatory/Legal – show readiness for implementation Training – show readiness for implementation Support – after go-live – show readiness for implementation Marketing campaigns – show readiness for implementation date Implementation planning – show readiness for implementation
Usual format	Microsoft Word document, but could be PowerPoint slides
Signed off by	Project Board

Project Closure Report

Produced by	Project Manager with inputs from whole project team
Use	Mainly to annotate lessons learned
Contents	What went well What went badly List of lessons learned Actions still to be completed
Usual format	Microsoft Word document
Signed off by	Project Manager and Project Board

Glossary

Agile – group of software development methods that promotes the development of solutions through collaboration between self-organizing, cross-functional teams.

Baselined – documents and products that are complete and subject to change control.

Budgetary estimate – an estimate produced without detailed facts to substantiate it. Used to help work out budgets, carefully caveated to make clear that it cannot be relied on.

Change Request – once documents or products are baselined, any changes must be made through a Change Request, to be approved by the project board.

CHAOS Report – produced by the Standish Group in 2014 using feedback from 365 people representing 8,380 software applications, this surveyed projects to ascertain the commonest causes of failure.

Contingency – days and/or time added to a project budget or timeframe to help mitigate project risks.

Gantt Chart – a representation of a project plan in a bar chart, as promoted by Henry Gantt in the early 20th century.

Microsoft Project – project planning software produced by Microsoft, formerly the ubiquitous tool for planning projects.

PID – Project Initiation Document. Produced in the start-up stage, this document summarizes the project.

PMP – Project Management Professional certification, a project management methodology devised by the Project Management Institute and an internationally recognized standard adopted worldwide.

PRINCE2 – Projects In Controlled Environments 2. A project management methodology devised by the UK Government, Office of Government Commerce as described in 'Managing Successful Projects with PRINCE2'. An internationally recognized standard adopted worldwide.

Project Board – the executive committee for a project.

Project Plan – visual aid showing the tasks and resources required to complete a project, typically a plan represented as a Gantt chart.

RAID Log – a document containing details of any Risks, Assumptions, Issues and Dependencies pertinent to the project.

Scrum – the most commonly adopted Agile development method.

SMB – Small or Medium Sized Business. Generally accepted by international standards to be a company with fewer than 250 staff.

SME – Small or Medium Sized Enterprise.

Senior User/Product Owner – owner of products being delivered by the project, typically the manager of a department who uses them.

Sponsor – a senior staff member with ultimate responsibility for the project, who delegates delivery responsibility to the project manager.

Sprint – a piece of work, of short duration, that delivers functionality in an Agile project.

User Stories – stated project requirements expressed in the form 'As a <role> I want <goal or action> to achieve <benefit>.'

Velocity – measure of the productivity of an Agile project.

Waterfall – method of project delivery where each stage 'flows' into the next, usually comprising requirements, design, build and test stages.

Index

Discounts

Rational Plan are offering a 10% discount on RationalPlan Single and Multi to readers of this book. Enter code PM-Results in the discount coupon box at the checkout. www.rationalplan.com

Easyprojects are also offering a 10% discount on their products to readers of this book. Enter code GrenPM10 in the coupon box at the checkout. www.easyprojects.net

An acknowledged expert in project management for SMBs, Gren Gale has dedicated his working life to managing projects of all sizes effectively and efficiently.

Before establishing his own company in the UK, he led numerous teams in small organizations and blue chips alike, coordinating and running local, national and international programs and change departments.

Founder and CEO of PM Results, a company set up to enable smaller businesses to implement world class project management practices, he is a Prince 2 practitioner and professional Scrum Master.

For more information visit **PMresults.co.uk**

ZANNAC

BOOKS

www.ingramcontent.com/pod-product-compliance
Lightning Source LLC
Chambersburg PA
CBHW060607200326
41521CB00007B/683